DISPELLING ILLUSION

SUNY Series in Religious Studies
Harold Coward, editor

DISPELLING ILLUSION

Gauḍapāda's "Alātaśānti"

with an Introduction

Douglas A. Fox

STATE UNIVERSITY OF NEW YORK PRESS

Published by
State University of New York Press, Albany

Printed in the United States of America

For information, address State University of New York Press, State University Plaza, Albany, NY 12246

Production by Christine Lynch
Marketing by Theresa A. Swierzowski

Library of Congress Cataloging-in-Publication Data

Fox, Douglas A., 1927–
Dispelling illusion : Gauḍapāda's Alātaśānti, with an introduction / Douglas A. Fox.
p. cm. — (SUNY series in religious studies)
"Alātaśānti" : p. 91–93.
Includes bibliographical references and index.
ISBN 0-7914-1501-5 (alk. paper). : ISBN 0-7914-1502-3 (pbk. : alk. paper)
1. Gauḍapāda Ācārya. Alātaśānti. 2. Advaita. I. Gauḍapāda Ācārya. Alātaśānti. English & Sanskrit. II. Title. III. Series.
B132.A3F69 1993
181'.482—dc20 92-24051
CIP

10 9 8 7 6 5 4 3 2 1

For Michael and Elizabeth

Contents

Acknowledgments ix

Preface xi

Part One: Historical and Critical Introduction 1

- Gauḍapāda 3
- Context 9
- Gauḍapāda and Buddhism 21
- Grounds of Conviction 41
- *Māṇḍūkya Upaniṣad* and Gauḍapāda's *Kārikās* 45
- Summaries of *Prakaraṇas* I, II, and III 51
- Principal Ideas in the Fourth *Prakaraṇa:* "Ālātaśanti" 59
- Arguments for *Ajāti* (non-production) 71

Part Two: The Text: Gauḍapāda's "Quenching the Firebrand" 77

- Introductory Note 79
- "Alātaśānti" 81

Part Three: Commentary 93

Notes 131

Bibliography 135

Index 143

Acknowledgments

I am grateful to many persons for encouragement in the project that has resulted in the present book. To the Colorado College for released time; to the University of Toronto for the opportunity to use its excellent Robarts Library; to professors Ronald Morton Smith and Stella Sandahl of the same university for their generous friendship during a sabbatical leave spent in their milieu; to my family, for their remarkable patience. Especially I wish to thank Mrs. Phoebe McReynolds who proved once more to be a kind friend and an efficient collaborator in bringing the manuscript to its final form.

Preface

Gauḍapāda is at once an enigma and a figure of extraordinary importance in the history of Indian philosophy. Scholars and devotees have argued vigorously—sometimes even rancorously—about whether he was a real person, a school of thought, or even simply a philosophical treatise. Further, they debate whether, if he existed, he was a Buddhist (or at least a crypto-Buddhist) or a Vedāntin. The importance of Gauḍapāda in Hindu thought, however, lies beyond these questions. He—or it—was said to be the mentor of Govinda, who, in turn, was Śaṅkara's *guru,* and one may seriously question whether the formidable accomplishments of the great Śaṅkara would have been possible without Gauḍapāda.

Gauḍapāda offers us a glimpse into a dramatic moment in Hindu philosophy: the beginning of the recovering from Buddhism of intellectual leadership for those who acknowledge the Vedas and, especially, the Upaniṣads as authoritative. This alone would make his work valuable for the intellectual historian, but he also offers us one of India's most concrete and accessible systems of non-dualism. Moreover, it is one in which both the enduring strength and the alleged weaknesses of this position can be seen with rare clarity. This makes him an invaluable introduction to Advaitic thought for even the novice.

Despite all this, Gauḍapāda has so far had a disappointing share of the attention of Western scholars.

One possible reason for his neglect is that he has not left us a large body of writing. Several extant works are traditionally ascribed to him, but only three seem to merit serious consideration: a *bhāṣya* on Īśvarakṛṣṇa's *Sāṁkhya-kārikās*, a commentary on the *Uttaragītā*, and a *kārikā* on the *Māṇḍūkya Upaniṣad*. The last of these is generally the most valued of the set, and it must be doubted whether the others could be by the same hand as it.

The present work examines the *Māṇḍūkyakārikā*, but focuses on the fourth section after summarizing the earlier ones. The reason for this focus is that the final part (Alātaśānti) has the appearance of a separate and independent work, is a systematic essay on Gauḍapāda's version of non-dualism, and is the work above all in which he resorts to Buddhist terms to expound what seems to be a pre-Śaṅkaran Advaita. It is worth the attention of Western scholars because it is a watershed in Hindu philosophy, is engagingly controversial, and is fascinating as the expression of a powerful mind.

To assist our study, a fresh translation of the Alāta-śānti is offered, and this is surrounded by an historical introduction and a commentary. The introduction addresses critical issues, such as Gauḍapāda's relation to Buddhism, his *pramāṇas* (or "grounds of conviction") and his defence of the distinctive doctrine of *ajāti* (non-production). It attempts to place Gauḍapāda in context and to offer an overview of his ideas so that the text itself may be followed more easily. The commentary draws on Hindu and Western critical materials to explicate the meaning of the text in some detail.

Part One

HISTORICAL AND CRITICAL INTRODUCTION

GAUḌAPĀDA

History, it has been said with unconscious chauvinism, is the lengthened shadow of a man. The history of India's most celebrated system of religious philosophy may seem to confirm this, for it could be seen as the long shadow cast by a single and singular person: Gauḍapāda.

Other philosophies are more influential in the lives of India's masses, no doubt, but Advaita Vedānta has usually been honored, in recent centuries, as that country's supreme intellectual and spiritual achievement. It teaches that reality is not the confusing multiplicity we normally seem to see but, at root, a single One. It is, thus, non-dualist. And that One is not material but is ultimately a profound and perfect Consciousness. Armed with these ideas, the eminent Śaṅkara is said to have driven Buddhism from the fields of philosophical debate and to have established Advaita Vedānta as the most respected interpretation of the ancient wisdom of the Vedas, or scriptures, of India. *Advaita* means non-dualist and *vedānta* means the end or consummation of the *veda*, the inspired scriptures.

Śaṅkara's triumph is not in dispute, but to say that it was he who founded the Advaita philosophy in Hinduism is to go too far. He himself acknowledged his dependence on Gauḍapāda, whom he called his "*paramaguru*"—the teacher of his own *guru*, Govinda. Gauḍapāda, he said, had rescued the non-dualism (or monism) of the most important Upaniṣads (those richest of all Hindu scriptures) and had brought it to light again after dualist interpreters had buried it beneath their specious reasoning.

To study living Indian philosophy is inevitably to

study Advaita Vedānta, and to come to terms with this, to wrestle with its power and come to know what may be its weaknesses, it is to Gauḍapāda we should go first of all.

About Gauḍapāda the man we know, alas, almost nothing—perhaps nothing at all, since what we "know" may be wrong. To begin, even his name is an enigma for it is evidently not a real, personal name at all but a sort of nickname meaning something like "the worthy gentleman from Gauḍa." Gauḍa, or Gauḍadeśa (the Gauḍa region) lay in northern Bengal, and someone from there might be called Gauḍa. *Pāda*, although it means foot, was used sometimes as a title of respect, so some have speculated that our philosopher was a *sannyāsin*, one who had renounced the security of ordinary, secular life, given up his name and family, and devoted himself to spiritual perfection. This theory has it, then, that this scholar-saint became so respected that his disciples, not knowing his name, had to invent one for him and devised "Gauḍapāda" on the basis of the place he was known to have come from.

Of his life, we know little more. Ānandagiri, who wrote a commentary on the Gauḍapādan text we shall be examining, tells us something. Gauḍapāda lived and did penance (*tapasyā*) at a place named Badarikāśrama and there developed, or received by revelation, the Advaita philosophy.[1]

This "information" is so vague and impersonal that Max Walleser, among others, has even wondered whether such a person ever existed.[2] Perhaps "Gauḍapāda" refers not to an individual but to a school (as people in the United States might talk about "the Chicago School" in philosophy or Canadians about "the Group of Seven" in art). Or perhaps *pāda* is not an honorific suffix here but means a "step" or section in a book, so that "Gauḍapāda" really refers to the four chapters or segments of the work we shall examine and implies that it is a product of a school of thought centered in Gauḍadeśa.

The more we probe, the more Gauḍapāda imitates the Cheshire Cat—dissolving before our eyes with only an enchanted smile remaining, perhaps of derision. But when all the data are considered it seems most likely that Gauḍapāda was a real person. Śaṅkara's reference to him, and Ānandagiri's, certainly support this view, and the writings we can most surely believe to be his do not seem to be the work of a committee. They convey the warmth of a strong personality and a vigorous single mind. But when did he live?

The cat smiles again! If Śaṅkara lived in the eighth century, probably near its beginning as many recent studies suggest, and if Gauḍapāda was *guru* to Govinda who taught Śaṅkara, we must place him somewhere in or very near the seventh century. This may well be correct, but there is a problem.

It is clear that Gauḍapāda lived after the major Buddhist writers, especially Vasubandhu, whose work he clearly reflects; but in an early sixth-century work by Bhāvaviveka there seem to be direct quotations from Gauḍapāda, and if so we must place our man no later than the fifth century.

Is it possible that Śaṅkara did not mean that Gauḍapāda was literally his *paramaguru* but only that he was the most important influence on Govinda and through him on Śaṅkara himself (as one might say "I studied philosophy with Professor X, and, as you know, Hegel was his master")? Yes. Quite possible. Then we may consign Gauḍapāda to the fifth century.

Or perhaps not! It is also possible that Bhāvaviveka is not quoting Gauḍapāda at all, but that both of them made use of a common source which is now lost to us.

From all this we can rescue only this much: Gauḍapāda seems to have been an actual individual who lived between the fifth and eighth centuries and powerfully influenced Śaṅkara, changing the course of Indian philosophy. At least we may dismiss the most absurd suggestions about him, including one that he flourished as early as 3000 B.C.E.

Gauḍapāda did not leave us much writing. Several works are traditionally attributed to him, but after careful scrutiny only three remain serious possibilities. There is a *bhāṣya* on Iśvarakṛṣṇa's *Sāṁkhyakārikās,* a commentary on the *Uttaragītā,* and a *kārikā* on the *Māṇḍūkya Upaniṣad.*

To explore Gauḍapāda's fertile mind, then, we shall examine the Fourth Section of his *kārikā* on the *Māṇḍūkya.*

A *kārikā* may be a metrical interpretation and extension of a text, and Gauḍapāda's first section in his *Māṇḍūkyakārikā* is precisely this. It quotes the Upaniṣad and selectively develops it. But the remaining sections leave the Upaniṣad behind and pursue their own themes, although at first these are themes that emerge from the scripture. The fourth section is the most independent of all. As we shall see, this has aroused controversy because this final section seems to stand alone and some have argued that it is an independent work that has somehow become attached to the others. Moreover, in this section Gauḍapāda makes more use of Buddhist terms than he does elsewhere—so much so that some scholars think he may have been a crypto-Buddhist who merely made convenient use of a Upaniṣad. These are matters we shall discuss in more detail; it is enough for us now to note that it is the final segment of Gauḍapāda's so-called *Māṇḍūkyopaniṣad Kārikā* that we shall study, drawing on the earlier chapters as and if they are useful for clarification. By this means we shall confront all the major ideas with which Gauḍapāda equipped Śaṅkara.

First, however, we must take note of some of the questions that scholarship has raised or settled about Gauḍapāda and we shall try to outline his principal ideas. Then we shall present a translation of the fourth section (*prakaraṇa*), which is entitled *"Alātaśānti"* ("Peace to the Firebrand" or "Extinguishing the Firebrand"). Finally, we shall offer a brief commentary on parts of the translated text.

There are several English renderings of the *kārikā* (or *kārikās*: one may use a plural or treat the word as a collective noun), so that a new one probably needs justification. This is easily given. The others have now so far receded from view that something should be done to attract attention once more to Gauḍapāda. Again, earlier translations, however solidly founded on good scholarship, tended to reflect a bias toward one or other of the rival answers to critical questions; for instance, they make Gauḍapāda a blatant Buddhist or they virtually conceal his use of Buddhist terms. Some translations are so painstakingly literal that the result can scarcely be called English; others work so hard to make a meaning clear that Gauḍapāda's text is left far behind.

The present aim, therefore, is to take all former translations into consideration, to offer a work that is faithful to the most likely *meaning* in Gauḍapāda's mind, and yet to achieve reasonable clarity in English.

CONTEXT

Before we look directly at Gauḍapāda's work it may be useful to indicate briefly some features of the religious and intellectual context in which he appeared. We shall not attempt an intellectual history of India here, but shall try to suggest the climate of the debate to which he contributed so significantly.

Religious speculation and piety in India stretch back through many centuries until they are lost to us in the ages before anything found a permanent record in oral or literary traditions. Artifacts from the Harappa culture, which flourished around the middle of the second millennium B.C.E., suggest an early fertility cult centered in a divine mother, probably associated with the earth, and a sacred bull which may have represented the masculine and fertilizing sky. But no writing from this ancient time lends us clear information and even the vague speculation we permit ourselves may be mistaken. For most of India we have even less basis for guessing about the religious situation at this remote time.

Towards the end of the second millennium a new people who called themselves Āryans began to infiltrate the subcontinent from the north, and it is with them that our information about religion becomes richer. They began to compose poems which were collected and passed on orally from one generation to another in sets called Vedas, and from these we learn quite a lot about attitudes, beliefs and practices that became some of the most important seeds out of which grew later Hindu religious aspirations and convictions.

In the philosophically most important of these collections, called the *Ṛg Veda*, we may actually see a transition from a time when many gods were affirmed to one in which questions were raised about whether, after all, there might not be one supreme deity or even whether there might not be something even older than any of the gods.

We should not assume, of course, that the ordinary person worried much, if at all, about such questions. If we are to judge from the main thrust of the early Vedas, it would seem that religion was chiefly a rather optimistic attempt, largely through ritual, to ensure the favor of the gods, the quiescence of more uncongenial spirits whom we may think of as demons, and the expanding prosperity of the Āryan people.

In time, however, early myths about how and why the world had come into existence ceased to satisfy certain enquiring minds. Further, there came to prominence two ideas not found clearly in the Vedas: *samsāra*, the idea that life does not end with death but goes on to a rebirth in some new form, and *karma*, the theory that the form of the new life will be dependent on behaviors a person has chosen during the present or even a past life.

Karma is a very convenient explanatory notion. It settles easily questions of why one person is rich and another poor, one healthy and handsome and another sickly or ugly. Whatever our condition in this life, it is to be explained by actions (the literal meaning of *karma*) in a previous existence.

The origin of these two ideas is disputed. Many have sought to locate them in a pre-Āryan indigenous people because they seem so incompatible with the Āryan attitudes to life and death. Others, pointing out that Āryans tended to despise the native peoples and would be unlikely to borrow ideas from them, have thought they arose among the Āryans themselves and circulated at first as esoteric doctrines known only to initiates. What is clear is that, wherever they found birth, *samsāra* and *karma* colored Indian attitudes decisively after they found general acceptance. The pristine cheerfulness of the Vedic poems begins to give ground to a more troubled spirit as the harshness of life for many people made the prospect of a potentially endless sequence of such lives unacceptable.

Between the eighth and fourth centuries—a period Karl Jaspers called "axial"—there appeared in various parts of the world a surprising surge of new thought. Prophets in Israel, Zarathustra in Iran, early Taoists and Confucius in China, and some of ancient Greece's most illustrious philosophers all taught creatively at this time. And in India there emerged a class of thinkers, often men who had retired to the quiet of forest places, who began to teach ideas that are collected in *āraṇyakas*—"forest books." The most important of these new works were at last called Upaniṣads, and with these the ritualism and simple theology of the earlier scriptures is decisively abandoned.

In the Upaniṣads we find that *samsāra* and *karma* have been joined by ideas about a single creative God who is the source of all that exists; a being known as Prajāpati ("Lord of Creatures") in the *Ṛg Veda* becomes Brahmā, a deity who has remained to this day part of the Hindu pantheon. Other gods begin to assume prominence, too, while many disappear. But most significantly we now find the idea that the underlying reality is not a personal god but an impersonal absolute called Brahman. Most daring of all is the concept that the inner essence, the "self" or spirit, of the human (called *ātman*) is actually Brahman, so that all is really a measureless One. It is not clear how Upaniṣadic thinkers may commonly have related the experience of manyness with this notion of the One, but the obvious explanation must have been that particulars are not finally "real" in the sense that Brahman is, and may therefore be some sort of illusion. Certainly this became, in time, a popular theme.

It was in this same dynamic period, especially if we extend it to about 200 B.C.E., that the seeds were planted of the great Hindu philosophical systems, both those that are considered orthodox and those that are not.

Perhaps one can say that the culmination, for orthodox Hindus, of this entire development lies in the *Bha-*

gavad Gītā, which eventually became the most popular religious book in the land. We shall say a little more about philosophy shortly, but the *Gītā* proved to be such a powerful influence that a few words should be spent on it now; it will serve to illustrate some of the complexity of the intellectual scene in which Gauḍapāda appeared.

Scholars and devotees have frequently noted that it is very difficult to make the content of the *Gītā* perfectly consistent. For the devotee, this hardly matters because he or she tends to take from it what is wanted and to ignore the rest. But scholars have struggled to make it unambiguous. Frankly, this seems quite impossible and perhaps the most fruitful approach to it is that taken by the provocative but excellent Indologist, A. L. Basham and conveniently outlined in his lectures published as *The Origins and Development of Classical Hinduism.*[3]

The *Gītā* was inserted into the epic *Mahābhārata* and tells the story of a conversation between the warrior, Arjuna, and the God Viṣṇu, who is incarnated as Kṛṣṇa. Arjuna is about to engage in a terrible civil war to regain a kingdom which rightfully belongs to his brothers and himself, but before the battle he surveys the enemy and finds there relatives, teachers, former friends—people whom he ought to respect. In despair he throws down his weapon and announces to Kṛṣṇa that he would rather lose the kingdom, or even his own life, than be guilty of killing such persons. It is a sentiment that immediately appeals to many modern people.

Kṛṣṇa, however, tells him that he must fight in such a just cause, and briefly explains why. Then the *Gītā* launches into a long sermon by Kṛṣṇa which goes far beyond Arjuna's original question and deals with many issues of religious philosophy. In the course of this it sometimes appears that the deity is supreme and personal, and at other times the impersonal Brahman looms as the ultimate reality. Correspondingly, sometimes devotion to God is the highest act, and at other times it is the seeking of that knowledge in which all sense of otherness has vanished, so that there is no divine "other" to adore.

Sometimes one must act without regard to the outcome in order to lose any sense of individual selfhood and become pure Brahman, and at others one must act without regard to the outcome simply in devotion to God. How are we to reconcile these mutually exclusive ideas?

Basham's simple but plausible suggestion is to find three main authors of the work as it now stands. The first wrote only the short passage in which war is justified. The second was a non-dualist who believed that Brahman is all. The third was a devotee of Kṛṣṇa (or of Viṣṇu, of whom Kṛṣṇa is an *avatār*). The last poet composed not only whole sections, but shorter fragments which he inserted into the text left him by the non-dualist.

Whether this is really what happened or not, there certainly seem to be three segments of the work and they reflect the debate to which Gauḍapāda contributed. In the justification of war we find a voice that upholds the traditional Hindu teaching that one must act honorably in accordance with one's caste (that is, one's place in the social order) and since Arjuna was a warrior, he must fight. In the non-dualist we find the view that all historic endeavor is trivial because Brahman is all, and Brahman is without division. In the words of the theist we find that even if the term Brahman is useful, it is as a name for the "womb" from which God creates all that is. As we shall see, it is to the non-dualist position that Gauḍapāda gives his loyalty and in doing so he finds little use for theism and reduces even the traditional caste duties to a sphere where they are less than "real" in the sense that Brahman is real. Indeed, we shall find him extremely radical in his denial of events.

As we have said, an ingredient in this developing mixture was the emergence of schools of philosophy, and while it would take us too far from our purpose to attempt even a summary outline of their teachings, some comment may be useful.

The great systems probably arose partly because the Vedas, Upaniṣads, and other works so far produced were far from systematic or mutually consistent. How could one find a path through them to a vision of unambiguous truth?

There are often said to have been six orthodox and four heterodox systems. This is somewhat misleading because there were actually more, and even the customarily identified "schools" contained variations, but such subtleties need not detain us at present.

The six major orthodox schools of thought were the Nyāya, Vaiśeṣika, Sāṃkhya, Yoga, Mīmāṃsā and Vedānta and the most powerful heterodox rivals were Buddhism, Jainism, the Ājīvikas and various Materialists. Although all the orthodox teachers accepted the Vedic scriptures as authoritative, even among them there were significant differences of interpretation and opinion. For example, while all of them spoke of the need for appropriate behavior and usually meant behavior in accordance with one's caste and stage of life, the Mīmāṃsā was extraordinary in being a truly "activist" school. For it, the major objective of life was to discover how to act properly in order to achieve liberation from the afflictions of the usual *samsāric* round of unpalatable rebirths, and since it assumed that the Vedas were inspired to present us with the needed understanding, it tended to place enormous stress on accurate ritual performance in accordance with Vedic instructions and demands. By contrast the other schools tended to emphasize knowledge of some kind and, without eliminating it entirely, to reduce the dominance of ritual. Most schools asked of a text, what does it mean? The Mīmāṃsā asked, what does it imply that we should *do*?

Again, an important question concerned the nature of the individual self and its relation to whatever else exists. Here, once more, we find dissension. Sāṃkhya and Yoga saw the individual as pure and distinctive spirit, *puruṣa*, which needed liberation from the realm of matter and non-spirit (*prakṛti*) and the attainment of an eternal state of isolated perfection. Early Buddhism denied that there was really such a self to liberate, and the Vedāntic view (as developed by Gauḍapāda and others) held that there is only one immeasurable Self with no actual objective world outside it from which it could be liberated: there was only the illusion of such a world.

The desire for liberation, however, was one that united virtually all the schools. They agreed that life, as we know it, is infected by some kind of dissatisfaction. As Karl H. Potter has it, "There is a fundamental agreement among Indian philosophers of practically all persuasions about the basic problem of systematic philosophy. That problem, in a nutshell, is to discover a conceptual scheme or map in which we can find a route to complete freedom from wherever we are now."[4] On this question, materialists tended to argue for making the best of things because there is no hope of a deliverance into some new postmortem state. The Buddhist work, *Dīgha Nikāya* (1.55), apparently quotes one of these teachers, Ajita Keśakambalin, as saying that when death comes to the physical body the wise and the stupid share the same fate: they are simply eliminated with no hope of anything more. Other groups were more hopeful: those of them rooted in the belief in a personal God talked about the achievement of a perfect relationship with him or her, while those that denied the reality of God in favor of an impersonal ultimate spoke more about the attainment of an ideal state of being beyond all relationship.

Whatever form of liberation or liberated state was offered, however, the question always remained of the method for reaching it, and here again there was both agreement and disagreement. The Mīmāṃsā chiefly offered a path of obedient ritual behavior; the Buddhists talked about an "eightfold path" which included disciplines of body and mind, the holding of "right views," and the abandonment of all value judgments about oneself or anything else. The end of this path would be the loss of the illusion of our persisting individual selfhood and a corresponding relief from the alarms and anxieties that normally trouble us.

Perhaps in response to Buddhism, Patañjali provided his Yoga school and its near partner, Sāṃkhya, with a system of physical and mental control which had "eight limbs." This was a path as arduous as the Buddhist but was not directed toward the elimination of the inner self (*ātman* or *puruṣa*) but rather to its purification and separation from the psycho-physical in which it lay. The "limbs" included rules of behavior and restraint, mastering a suitable posture and control of breathing and, like the Buddhist way, withdrawing attention from objects and holding the mind steady until it became a pure and contentless consciousness.

While also favoring meditation, the Jains added a flavor of their own. Like other schools, they held that we are spirits entrapped in matter. Moreover, the entire world is full of such spirits in various intensities of entrapment. Humans and some of the "higher" animals are actually relatively free and can strive toward total liberation, but other animals, plants, and even rocks also have souls that are so encrusted with matter that they can do little but wait for time to ease the pressure upon them. Our present state (and many of the schools would have echoed this) is the result of *karma*—the principle that our deeds have consequences for the state of our future living. Since the worst form of action, for the Jain, was violence, the ideal (in addition to meditation) was so to live that we reduce as much as possible the violence we do to other beings. Thus the Jain monk was supposed to walk slowly and even to brush softly the path before him lest he step on some tiny creature. He had to do without fire because this might kill an insect or injure the air; he could own no property, not even clothing or a begging bowl, but must beg for his food with cupped hands. There were other restrictions of this kind, and it is obvious that they could be endured by only the most serious. Jain laypersons were generally satisfied with less arduous discipline.

Despite their differences, virtually all the schools referred to held one idea in common: our behavior and our life in general might be largely shaped by past *karma*, but there is always some measure of freedom available to us. Otherwise, they would have said, there is nothing we can do to liberate ourselves.

Precisely! said the Ājīvikas. This school was so distasteful to its rivals that it has vanished and even its scriptures are now known to us only through the pejorative writings of others. But it seems that it taught that a force called *niyati* (which means "destiny") so completely determines all that we are and all that we do that no freedom of self-determination exists. However, we are not without hope because the natural process in which we are helplessly swept along will, in time (a great deal of time!), bring us to deliverance from its own clutches.

That life is imperfect and that a pathway to liberation from all that troubles us is desirable, all seem to have accepted—expect, perhaps, the various Materialists. But whose analysis of the problem and the path was correct? Or did this not matter?

To find the right way was obviously of great concern to orthodox Hindu and heterodox thinkers alike, and we find the repeated warning that no discipline of mind or body will bring true freedom if it is built on a wrong understanding. But how may we determine which system offers the *right* understanding?

Each of the schools defended its own position vigorously, and one of the conventional ways of doing so was to indicate what it held to be means of true or valid knowledge (*pramāṇas*). All told, there were about six of these, but some were peculiar to one or two schools while others were more generally accepted. We shall discuss those used by Gauḍapāda soon, but meanwhile we shall focus on the *pramāṇa* "perception" because this will help us to capture the general tenor of the debate and to see where Gauḍapāda fits in it.

When we speak of knowledge we generally think of a knower (or subject), what is known (the object) and the state of knowing. Indian philosophy began with the same assumption. Knowledge is a relation between *viṣaya*, a subject, and *viṣayin*, an object.

But how can we be sure of this? Is it possible that knowledge is a quality of the knower and not a relation at all because there is no object outside the knower's own mind (that is, outside the "knowing") at all?

Nyāya faced this question. Perception, it held, was a major source of true and dependable knowledge, but only when the perception was attended by understanding of the object. If I saw something but did not know what it was, this could hardly be the kind of perception that contributed to knowledge.

Very well, but we all know that we make perceptual mistakes. We see a mirage and think it is a pond or, to use the common Indian example, we see what we think is a snake, but on second glance see it to be no more than a harmless coil of rope. If mistakes like these occur, how can we trust perception ever to bring us authentic knowledge?

Test the perception, said various schools. Act as if the perception were accurate and see what happens. If our behavior "works," then we are entitled to assume the perception is true. Ah, but is not the perception that the behavior has "worked" itself only one more perception? Must we then test that, and so go on and on testing new hypotheses *ad infinitum*? Mīmāṃsā thought this absurd, and most of the 'realistic' schools agreed. If the conditions of accurate perception were present (enough light, and so on) then it makes best sense to test the perception pragmatically, and trust it without further bother until and unless something happens to challenge it. You cannot go on testing forever!

But is there any way to account for *mis*perception? Why do I momentarily mistake a rope for a snake? How can I perceive a snake when there is none present? Many philosophers found this easy to answer. A snake is not present now, but a snake *has been* present to me at some time, and I then had a true perception of it. My problem is that, for a moment, I have had an unsolicited memory of that snake as I glanced at the rope. The snake perception was correct and the rope perception is accurate, but the mistake occurred when I replaced the perception true at the moment with one that was true at some earlier time. In other words, the problem is not with perception but with the unwanted intrusion of a memory.

Another question came to mind. When we perceive an

object, do we perceive the thing-itself or merely its qualities? I look at and handle an apple: a shape is seen, and color; a texture is felt; an aroma and flavor are experienced, and as a result of this we say, "This is an apple"—but have we really perceived an apple or only the various qualities that we associate with apples?

In Europe, questions of this kind led David Hume and others to argue that we never really know the "substance" behind qualities, so have no reason whatever to accept the idea that substance exists. The usual Indian answer was different. Our senses perceive only qualities, it is true, but as they operate we somehow directly intuit the thing-itself. This does not seem to have been an idea very carefully or thoroughly explored, but rather one accepted as axiomatic.

The concept of perception and knowledge that we have roughly sketched so far did not satisfy all inquirers. In the first place, what if perception were, after all, merely something belonging to the subject, to the "perceiver"? What if it was purely subjective and there really is nothing "out there" corresponding to it? How could one prove the matter one way or the other? And why would one choose to insist that there are objects to be known, or why would one choose to dismiss them as unreal?

No doubt realists thought that it makes more sense of experience to say that the perception of an apple arises when an apple is present. But it is impossible to prove this. If you say, "my friend and I both agreed that the thing was there—we both saw and touched the apples," I might reply that your perception of your friend and his agreement is as unreliable as the perception of the apple! There might be only the perception in your mind of apple and friend and common experience.

To live successfully in the world, however, it is easier to assume that perceptions are generally true and an objective world exists. But if living in the world is not something one much desires, success in it may not count for much. So we may ask, why would one prefer the alternative, the view that there are no real objects, only subjectivity? The answer is immediate: if, as we know, Upaniṣadic wisdom saw that "fear comes from otherness," then to abandon belief in objects is to abandon otherness and to rise above fear! A nightmare starts to lose its power the moment we begin to realize that it is only a dream. What if the entire threatening world is only a dream?

Then, if our other question—whether we perceive real objects or only their qualities—is answered as it often was, a new thought may arise. We perceive only qualities but infer the object. But what if we could cease to perceive qualities altogether? What then? Could it be that the "Real" appears to our awareness not through qualities, but when we stop paying attention to qualities? If we stop believing in objects outside ourselves and cease to attend to qualities, ordinary perception comes to an end. We are left with a state of consciousness that contains nothing yet is not a mere unconsciousness. This utterly untroubled state may be the "perception" of what really *is*—and since we no longer objectify ourselves, it is also what we really are. The true "I" is *ātman*, pure spirit, and *ātman* is Brahman, the all.

With ideas like these Gauḍapāda recaptured what he thought were some of the most important truths of the Upaniṣads. Fear is false because there is no "other" to fear. Brahman, the ultimate reality, is *ātman*, my true self. There is no other at all! But to know my true self, and therefore simply to be Brahman, I must stop paying attention to the qualities that bombard my senses; they are not qualities of anything real—and therefore they are not themselves real.

Gauḍapāda, thus, established a position outside other schools of thought, but in doing so felt that he had truly understood all that really mattered in Indian thought—orthodox or heterodox.

Now we must turn to the man himself.

GAUḌAPĀDA AND BUDDHISM

No one disputes the fact that Gauḍapāda makes some use of Buddhist terms. Yet he also uses Upaniṣads and goes so far as to offer *kārikās* on one. Was he, then, a crypto-Buddhist, perhaps seeking to seduce the unwary by making heresy sound like an acceptable tradition? Is he a true Vedāntist, a faithful son of the Vedas who uses Buddhist language only because it is convenient? Or is there some other explanation?

This question may seem drily academic: what can it possibly matter, so long after the event, to what system Gauḍapāda gave his loyalty? The fact is, it obviously matters quite a lot to certain people, and even among competent scholars (whom we may expect to value objectivity) partisan attitudes are sometimes expressed with astonishing passion.

If we confront fairly recent scholarship with the question whether Gauḍapāda was a Buddhist rather than a Vedāntin we find quite an array of answers. Surendranath Dasgupta says Yes; T. M. P. Mahadevan says No; Sarvepalli Radhakrishnan says Maybe; Vidhushekhara Bhattacharya says he was a Vedāntin in loyalty, but what he actually taught was Buddhism; T. R. V. Murti says he certainly was a Vedāntin, and he did not actually *teach* Buddhism but used Buddhist terms as a tool to reformulate Upaniṣadic ideas. R. D. Karmarkar stoutly maintains that Gauḍapāda is not only a Vedāntin, and a faithful one, but one who really does not use Buddhist terms so very much after all, and when he does it is for the purpose of discrediting Buddhist notions.

The wildly dialectical nature of this debate is nicely

illustrated by two translations of Gauḍapāda's major work, the *kārikās* on the *Māṇḍūkya* (or, as it is also called, the *Āgama-śāstra*). Vidhushekhara Bhattacharya has offered one of these, and in it, as well as in his notes, he labors to reveal Gauḍapāda's heavy dependence on Buddhist sources. R. D. Karmarkar was evidently incensed by this, and prepared a translation of his own which conceals much of the evidence for Buddhist influence. In his commentary he traduces Bhattacharya frequently, and on the whole he manages to give the impression that Gauḍapāda's use of familiar Buddhist words was only incidental or pejorative. Their contest is best illustrated by their respective treatment of verse 99.

My own rendering of this verse is: "According to the enlightened one [which might or might not be a reference to the Buddha] understanding [*jñānam*] never touches objects, and no object touches understanding. The Buddha has not said this."

In its context, the meaning of the verse seems clear. The Buddha, or enlightened persons as a class, understands that there is no actual, direct contact between a mind or consciousness and an object: the mind knows only images or ideas. It is not polluted by the immediate presence of real things. But the last sentence is a problem.

"*Na itad Buddhena bhāṣitam*": The Buddha has not said this. This is grammatically simple, but what does it mean?

Karmarkar has no difficulty here. He writes, "What Gauḍapāda means to say is that Gautama Buddha told many things...but he could not grasp the *ajātivāda* which is the only proper solution to the problem of *samsāra*.[5]

This is a confident interpretation, but surely a little odd. The verse says nothing directly about *ajātivāda* (Gauḍapāda's doctrine that no real entity is ever brought into existence) or *samsāra* (the cycle of reincarnation). These are, however, at the center of Gauḍapāda's teaching, and it is important to Karmarkar to have our sage remark that he did not learn these things from the Buddha.

By contrast, Bhattacharya sees the issue quite differently. "The Buddha has not said this"? Of course! Many Buddhist sources tell us repeatedly that the Buddha often refused to say something. Take the popular *Laṅkāvatāra Sūtra* for example. It says, "It is said by the Blessed One that from the night of the enlightenment until the night of the Parinirvāṇa [i.e. his death] the Tathagata [Buddha] in the meantime has not uttered even a word, nor will he ever utter; for not-speaking is the Buddha's speaking."[6]

In other words, the Buddha was often silent when faced with questions, and his silence was not a mere refusal to answer the question, but the perfect answer. When we confront issues that take us beyond the reach of words and concepts, silence is the only correct speech. Therefore, according to Bhattacharya, what Gauḍapāda means to do here is to pay tribute to the Buddha, and to say that whatever he, Gauḍapāda, knows about the relation of consciousness and objects he has learned from the Buddha's silence.

For Karmarkar, then, Gauḍapāda learned all he knew from orthodox, Vedāntic sources and explicitly repudiated the Buddha. For Bhattacharya, he wanted to be a Vedāntist, but had learned so much from Buddhism that it shaped even his reading of the Upaniṣads.

Where does the truth lie? What value might there be in finding an answer to such a question?

It will be the contention of the next few pages that even if we cannot reach a conclusive answer to our question, we can find a plausible hypothesis that we may use with some confidence. Further, if this hypothesis is true, it gives us a useful clue to some of the motivation in much religious behavior and, even more important, an insight into a perennial human quest. To understand why someone has behaved as he or she did, why they reached certain attitudes and values, may be a key to the difficult and sometimes alarming question, why am *I* as I am?

What follows here may be tedious to any but Indologists and Sanskritists, and all too familiar to them, but it is important for the establishing of the promised hypothesis. Selectively and illustratively we shall draw upon traditional sources to argue that the focus of Gauḍapāda's loyalty was the Vedānta, but the main source of his most important ideas lay in Buddhism. Then we shall ask why he may have joined these two traditions as he did, and the answer will be the root of our hypothesis about human behavior, philosophy, and religion.

Ajātivāda, the doctrine that there is no birth or production of substantial or fully "real" things anywhere or at any time, and therefore no "real" objective world outside consciousness, is central to Gauḍapāda. But if this is true, we have to account for our evidently mistaken experience of things. We certainly *seem* to see, touch, smell, hear and taste a world. If there is none, how can this be? The answer Gauḍapāda gives is founded in the concept of *māyā*: illusion. All sensory and mental experience, except the experience of contentless consciousness, is illusion.

It will serve our present purpose if it can be shown that Gauḍapāda's use of these terms and the ideas they represent is not to be found fully formed in the Vedānta literature before him, but is to be discovered in Buddhist materials that he gives evidence of knowing.

In scanning Vedāntic sources we may omit the *Brahmasūtras* because Gauḍapāda never quotes them and no one claims that they were an influence on his system. We shall, in fact, confine ourselves to the sources he may be expected to have learned his ideas from: the older Upaniṣads and the *Bhagavad Gītā*.

The *Gītā* is easily disposed of. I can find only four times when the idea of non-birth (*aja*) occurs there. In II.20 we read that Kṛṣṇa is unborn, eternal and everlasting in his *ātman*. In IV.5–6 Kṛṣṇa tells Arjuna, "You and I have gone through many births....Even though my *ātman* is birthless and changeless, I was born through my own power." Here again it is the deity who is unborn in essence (or *ātman*), not Arjuna or others. In the remaining references, VII.25 and X.3, we find the same thing: the divine is unborn, but in this it is unique.

The term *māyā* also occurs sparingly in the *Gītā*—four times—but it does not seem to bear the suggestion of "illusion" that it has for Gauḍapāda except vaguely and in one place. In IV.6 Kṛṣṇa says that he is born "by my own power" (*ātma-māyāya*), and there is no obvious need to regard this power or what it achieves as an illusion. In VII.14–15 *māyā* is once again used to mean power, and this power seems securely tied to the realm of matter when we are told that it is "composed of the *guṇas*." In VII.24 we learn that Kṛṣṇa is concealed or disguised by "*yoga-māyā*" and this does suggest an element of deception in the power that is *māyā*, but the point being made is that humans are deceived by this power, not that humans and their world are illusions. Finally, XVIII.61 offers us *māyāya* again, but as the term for the power by which Kṛṣṇa moves us as if we were puppets.

The *Gītā*, then, gives us the words we seek but not the meaning that Gauḍapāda assigned to them. As Dasgupta has it, "It is evident that Gītā does not know the view that the world may be regarded as a manifestation of māyā or illusion."[7]

We turn, then, to the early Upaniṣads. The very influential *Bṛhadāraṇyaka* presents us with a rather remarkable idea. At first, we are told, there was only Brahman, but in its isolation it was unproductive (*na vyabhavat*). Then Brahman began to create the rulers among the gods (I.iv.11).

The suggestion here is that Brahman is the ground and even the agent of creation (as we would say, the material and efficient causes) and there is no indication that the creation is insubstantial.

In II.iii.1–6 we discover that there are two aspects of this ultimate Brahman, the formed and the formless. The first of these consists of all that is mortal and finite, and the latter is the infinite immortal itself. The mortal is obviously less ultimate than the other; it exists "so to speak" (*iva*), but this probably means only that it is dependent and secondary.

How, in this text, does the One (Brahman) become, even temporarily, expressed in the many? We are offered a suggestion: *indro māyābhiḥ puru-rūpa īyate*—"the deity by his *māyā* goes in many forms." Here *māyā* seems to mean power, a power to transform oneself without thereby necessarily becoming any less than one intrinsically is. This is not yet the *māyā* of Gauḍapāda.

Of this ultimate *Ātman* itself, Brahman, the *Bṛhadāraṇyaka* is clear that it is "unborn" (IV.iv.20–25) and the term here is Gauḍapāda's beloved *aja*.

So Brahman transforms itself into the forms of the world, yet in itself remains singular; as IV.iv.19 says, "There is no plurality whatever here."

Thus we have an irreducible essential unity, but a unity that can take a variety of forms simultaneously. This may be the root of an idea that the forms are illusion, but that is still far from explicit.

When we move to the *Katha* we find another startling image: the supreme *Ātman* is "bodiless among bodies" (*aśarīram śarīresu*) in I.ii.22 and it takes its seat in the heart of every creature (I.ii.20). The great error of the unenlightened is to see the multiform character of the world as if it were final and irreducible, to assume that *Ātman* itself must be many. "Whoever sees here multiplicity passes through death after death" (II.i.10).

But perhaps the clearest picture presented by this *Upaniṣad* of the relation of supreme *Ātman* and the many earthly forms is given in II.ii.1: "The unborn, unbent intelligence [dwells in] a city with eleven gates." This gated city is, of course, the body and it is the indwelling intelligence that is unborn, not the body. In fact, this *Upaniṣad* speaks in several places as if the *Ātman* were an eternal spirit which associates with personal, individual spirits who, although transient, are possessed of some independent reality (cf. II.ii.12 and II.ii.13 where we find the phrase "the conscious amid the conscious").

So far, then, we seem to find a Brahman who is one but elects not to be solitary. *Māyā* is a term meaning the power of this ultimate being to bring dependent beings into existence, and although some *māyā* may produce confusion and deception, there is no reason to say that the substantial world produced by it is only a dream. But Brahman alone has aseity; Brahman alone is "unborn."

This position is not changed by the *Muṇḍaka*, one of the few remaining Upaniṣads that we may suppose Gauḍapāda to have known. It tells us in II.i.2 that Puruṣah, the primal being, is *ajāh*, unborn, but from him issue life, mind, the senses, ether, air, light, earth and, following these, all creation. Once again the born emerges from the unborn, but there is no hint of falsity about the appearance of things.

Indeed, among the Upaniṣads that Gauḍapāda is likely to have known, only one lends itself in any measure to a view like his own, and this is the one *Upaniṣad* we would not have expected a monist like him to approve because it is the eminently theistic *Svetāśvatara*.

Brahman is here sometimes identified with Rudra, the old Vedic god, and is said to be both the material and efficient causes of the world (cf. especially section III). The term *māyā* is used in this connection, but seems to mean only the divine creative power (cf. I.8).

However it is in this *Upaniṣad* that we find the idea that *all things* are fundamentally of a birthless nature. I.9 says, "There are two unborn ones, having and not having authority. Onc unborn is joined to the things that are to be experienced by the experiencer, and the self has no beginning (end)."[8]

This is rather obscure; what are we to make of it? It seems to suggest that the "self" or Brahman is unborn, but so is the sphere of unauthoritative experiencers and their objects of experience. The verse continues: "For the one who has all forms is not an actor/initiator. When one finds for one's self this trio, that is Brahma."

If the unborn is both Brahman and the world, yet it would seem that Brahman, the human experiencer, and the objects experienced form a trio which is not other than Brahman Itself, yet Brahman in its distinctive character initiates nothing; the creative impulse exists within Brahman as part of the "trio" but is not the nature of the ultimate and inclusive Brahman.

It is difficult to explicate this passage with great confidence. Śaṅkara would doubtless see the meaning here as his favorite doctrine: Brahman is All, and particulars are no more than illusory images superimposed on Brahman. Rāmānuja, on the other hand, understands the text pan-en-theistically: God or Brahman is the Ground and Power of our quite sufficiently real particular existences. As St. Paul is supposed to have told an Athenian audience, "In Him (God) we live and move and exist." Further, since Brahman (or God) is unborn, so is our power to be—but not our existence within that power. We exist within the divine, but not as it.

A verse later, in I.10, we hear that by meditating on Brahman we may be delivered from *viśva-māyā*, and it would be churlish to translate this as other than "world-illusion." Have we here, then, a clear anticipation of Gauḍapāda's view, the real source of his inspiration? The question is whether he or anyone else who read this text could legitimately understand it to mean that the world *is* an illusion (as Gauḍapāda will be saying) or merely that it fosters one. Are we deceived into thinking there is an actual world, or are we deceived in what we think *about* the actual world?

If we go a little further we find a clue to the Upaniṣad's intention. In II.15 we find that it is by knowing God that we may be liberated from bondage, and that this occurs when we perceive the truth about Brahman and ourselves. But what is this truth? II.16 gives it to us: "Here is God in all directions; born first indeed he is in the womb/embryo. He only born and going to be born stands against men facing everywhere."[9]

This must mean that God is all-pervasive: he is within the embryo, he has been born, and he will be born. In other words, God is the one who is birthless in essence, who is nevertheless present in all births. Despite this omnipresence, God remains "other" (*anyam*), as we learn in II.6, and we must recognize him in order to be set free (IV.7).

It is still not clear, therefore, that this Upaniṣad, any more than the others, discounts the reality of the world or reduces it to illusion. It does, evidently, place it within

God, but that is a typical form of sophisticated theism and is not necessarily close to Gauḍapāda's absolutism in which all origination of things is illusion and Brahman, the All, is not a deliberate world creator.

As if to confirm our view that the *Svetāśvatara* upholds the reality of the world within God, we hear in III.7 that God is "Enveloper of everything" (*pariveṣṭitāram*).

There are certain late Upaniṣads which present the term *māyā* in Gauḍapāda's sense (e.g., the *Subāla* and *Praśna*) but it is unreasonable to suppose these influenced Gauḍapāda (indeed, he may have influenced them).

We can see, then, that the Upaniṣadic tradition knew about the unborn character of the supreme reality and already indicated in a few places that *māyā* was a power that could deceive. What *māyā* produces, that which is born, may exist tenuously, but generally there is no question of its being unreal or mere appearance. I must therefore agree with P. V. Bapat when he says,"the non-origination theory, as applied to the phenomenal world, was unknown in Advaitism before Gauḍapāda."[10] And as for *māyā*, S. C. Chakravarti may not go too far when he says "the doctrine of māyā which Gauḍapāda develops could never have been taken from the older Upanishads."[11]

Did he, then, learn these ideas from Buddhist writings? At least two Buddhist schools appear to have been known to him: the Mādhyamika and the Vijñānavāda, and in the writings of both we find not only *māyā* in Gauḍapāda's sense of "illusion" but his "unborn" (*aja*) together with synonyms such as *anutpanna* (unarisen) and *anutpāda* (unborn or unproduced).

Mādhyamika's conviction was that the philosophical quest for ultimate truth is unavailing because it depends on the power of human minds to form adequate concepts and effective speech. Every concept is as limited as the human intelligence itself and cannot, therefore, reach what the metaphysician seeks. So Mādhyamika devoted its philosophy to the destruction or discrediting of ideas and systems of thought, showing that all lead, if pursued far enough, to an inevitable contradiction. In the end the mind must abandon the rationalist enterprise and admit defeat. This is the moment when, with thought-processes suspended, the wordless and inconceivable truth will simply appear, to be recognized immediately. It will be the truth the seeker *is*, and never a truth he or she knows *about*.

Mādhyamika, therefore, liked to use the term *śūnyatā* to point to this truth-beyond-conception. It was an "emptiness": not a nothingness but a no-thing-ness. There were no words for it, no possible valid ideas of it. The road to it lay in abandoning all ideas and all words, clinging to nothing in the mind, for every item of our thought stood between the truth and us. Let us not say "Brahman" or "*Ātman*" as if these named the final truth and supreme reality. These are words and, like all words, they will capture the imagination and block the truth. Let us not say even "Buddha" or "Nirvāṇa," for these words and ideas will do the same. It is to wordlessness we must go, beyond the very edge of thought. When that point is reached, there will be a truth to *be* but not to think.

There were two main instruments in the Mādhyamika repertoir: logic and meditation. The meditation was designed to awaken the practitioner to immediate, intuitive apprehension of truth when all false ideas (that is, *all* ideas) had been sufficiently suspended. The logic was a method for exposing the inadequacy of all propositions and concepts.

The logic is generally called a dialectic, and it operated to show that there are never more than four possibilities concerning any object of belief: it is so, it is not so, it both is and is not so, and it neither is nor is not so. When each of these options was shown to lead to contradiction, it was held that the targeted doctrine or proposition was invalid and must be abandoned. If the believer then leapt to an alternative, *that* too must be subjected to the fourfold critique and demolished.

Nāgārjuna was the foremost philosopher of early Mādhyamika, and in his hands the dialectic *(catuṣkoṭi)* proved devastating. He managed to dismiss even the seemingly inevitable notion of cause and effect by means of it. He showed that cause could not be the same as effect because if it were there would be no change and, therefore, no effect to speak of. Nor could it be different—truly something "other"—for if it were there could be no inevitable connection and any "effect" might follow from any "cause" in random fashion. Indeed, in such a situation the so-called "cause" could hardly be said to be the cause at all. But it is equally impossible to make sense of the idea that cause and effect are at once both the same and different, for nothing can be constructed of contradictory characteristics. Finally, one surely cannot say that cause and effect are neither the same nor different, for this would mean that no relation existed, and in that case every effect would have to be self-generated, which is absurd.

Mādhyamika, in this way, discredited all positive statements of metaphysics. Its critical and erosive dialectic was the heart of its philosophy. Yet one must not think it was nihilistic, although this was an accusation levelled by its critics, including Śaṅkara, and it is still occasionally echoed in our day.[12]

It will be easy to see that Gauḍapāda had certain things in common with the Mādhyamikans. We find him echoing their dialectic when he attacks causality, and it is this that enables him to reach his most important doctrine, *ajātivāda* or non-production. He shared other things with them, too, such as the recognition that the sphere of speech and ordinary knowledge is lower than the apprehension of truth itself—that there are two tiers or levels of understanding. And, of course, he used many Buddhist terms, even the distinctive "*nirvāṇa*." Indeed, some verses of Nāgārjuna sound as if they could have been written by Gauḍapāda, for instance, "origination, existence and destruction are all of the nature of *māyā*—dreams or castles in the air."[13]

Nevertheless, Gauḍapāda was, in the end, more positive in his statements than Mādhyamikans generally liked to be. Thus he did not rest content with the idea that all is "empty" (*śūnya*) of determining characteristics and nothing can be said about the highest reality. Instead he embraced the old terms (rejected by the Buddha) *ātman* (the self) and Brahman (the Absolute) and, like certain Upaniṣads he identified the *ātman* with Brahman. Indefinable they might be, but they were terms that pointed to a reality far too positive to justify a term like *śūnyatā*. Brahman was no emptiness; rather it was a fullness, and if one could show that the Mādhyamikan emptiness and Gauḍapāda's fullness really amounted to the same, still there is a significance in the fact that one side fled from the positive affirmation and the other embraced it.

A complete analysis of the relation between Gauḍapāda and Mādhyamika Buddhism would need more space and detailed attention than we give it here; but enough has been said to make a point. Gauḍapāda borrowed a logical method, some terminology, and at least some facets of the Mādhyamikan vision. But he preferred Vedic and Upaniṣadic rootage for his life and thought, even if his grasp of this rootage was often colored by Mādhyamikan caution.

The other major Buddhist school with which Gauḍapāda shows acquaintance is Vijñānavāda. This had begun with the Mādhyamikan recognition that ordinary knowledge is false and the truth is unreachable by means of the feeble constructions of our intellect, but it had wrestled with the problem of accounting for the arising both of those constructions and of the intellect itself, and had been led to some decisive innovations in philosophy.

Above all, the Vijñānavādins introduced a far more positive idea of the Absolute: this was no longer an emptiness, but Mind. It was *citta-mātra*: mind-only or pure mind. This meant that the Mādhyamikans had spoken truly when they said that the things of the world were insubstantial, but they might have been more helpful if they had recognized that the multiplicity of objects is a flowing complex of ideas, without any ground of their own, without independence, without endurance, without substance, but arising within and dependent on that pure mind or consciousness which bore them but was never divided or contaminated by them.

A functional metaphor represented the Mind (which we shall capitalize henceforth to remind ourselves that it is a universal and not a personal, individual reality) as a storehouse of seeds, the seeds of events, forces, and entities, which await the impulse of *karma* to germinate and have their hour. They are not outside the Mind; they are not even other than the Mind; but they are no less actual while they survive than are the ideas in our human minds. Pain is real while it is felt, and it is felt while the pained idea persists. Peace comes when ideas are allowed to fade until where they appeared to be there is only the perfect Mind itself, free of all thought and experience, free even of the divisive experience of self-recognition.

To know one is at peace is not to be at peace. To be at peace is to have no objective content in our mind, and in addition to techniques of meditation, the Vijñānavāda might borrow Mādhyamikan logic for the purpose of disavowing the credibility of all objects and all plurality. Consciousness then remained supreme—but this is a positive thing and need not be made opaque by obscure terms such as *śūnyatā*.

From the Vijñānavādin point of view it is clear that the things we humans encounter in the world are as real, but no more so, than the things we meet in dreams: both, in fact, are dreams, and the only difference is that one is a dream that a dream is dreaming! Even the Mādhyamikans had used the experience of realistic dreams to argue that waking experience could not prove the reality of objects, but in Vijñānavādin hands this became even more potent.

The Mādhyamikans had employed negation for the sake of removing all concepts and leaving consciousness empty and free. The Vijñānavādins had a more positive goal in mind. If an entity we experience does not "really" exist, then *something* certainly exists. The Mādhyamikans thought all concepts were contradictory. Yes indeed, said the Vijñānavādins, but there has to be something to entertain a contradiction, and this is a mind. But beneath the individual contradiction-laden minds of the world, as their sole reality, lay Mind-only.

As we go through some of Gauḍapāda's thought we will find many reflections of Vijñānavāda. So much is this true that Vidhushekhara Bhattacharya can say that although Gauḍapāda is a Vedāntin, yet "it is true that he advocates the Vijñānavāda."[14]

Is Gauḍapāda, then, a Vijñānavāda Buddhist? I think not. He may well have had a mind shaped largely by Vijñānavāda modes of thought and by Mādhyamikan critical analysis, but he was truly a Vedāntin in loyalty, and he used his thought to work with the material of certain Upaniṣads. It is true that, so far as we know, he used only one very short Upaniṣad as a direct basis for exposition (and that a late one which some have thought he may himself have written), but there is no mistaking his dependence also on at least the *Bṛhadāraṇyaka* and perhaps also the *Chāndogya*.

Examples of this dependence may be found in the teaching, in the *Bṛhadāraṇyaka*, of Yājñavalkya that the *ātman* is the reality of all, even though it remains perpetually undivided, or of the same sage's teaching that the true self underlies the three ordinary states of consciousness: wakefulness, dream, and dreamless sleep. There are other resemblances and often what seem to be direct quotations, but we are being suggestive, not exhaustive, in this analysis.

We are led to conclude, however tentatively, that Gauḍapāda was steeped in Buddhist teaching but saw himself as within the orthodox tradition that sprang from the Vedāntic sources. This position was probably not as uncomfortable as it might have been at an earlier stage of Buddhism because in Mādhyamika, Vijñānavāda and other developments, Buddhism itself undoubtedly had been taking a steady turn toward Upaniṣadic understanding. No doubt it is this that leads R. D. Ranade to say, "Instead of Gauḍapāda being a Pracchanna Buddha (a crypto-Buddhist) Nāgārjuna may be regarded as a Pracchanna Advaitin."[15]

But why, then, is there such a fuss about whether Gauḍapāda is a Buddhist or a Vedāntin? The answer, I suspect, is also the proper response to the question, why did Gauḍapāda finally affirm Vedāntic scriptures? It may be a matter of authority, or of the natural human longing for its assurance. Let us pursue this a little.

The Buddha had notoriously repudiated or neglected the Vedic materials, the *śruti* or established scriptures of the orthodox. In doing so he had based his teaching on the authority of his own inner vision. While few Indians have been inclined to question the significance of powerful subjective experience, and altered states of consciousness are sometimes uncritically accepted as foundations of belief, the *śruti* has a special place in Brahmanical commitment. It lies outside the subjectivity of the contemporary individual, and comes from an antiquity that places its origin beyond judgment. It can be held by faith, therefore, to be revealed truth or truth's own self-revealing—eternal and authorless.

Moreover, the importance of *śruti* lay not only in its antiquity and its supposed divinity, but in its essential changelessness, for in India the assumption that the eternal and true is static has had a very long history. As Ronald Morton Smith has pointed out, even the king's authority was most assured when it rested on a law that had Vedic support: "We are not going to have any personal or arbitrary ideas that may be reversed tomorrow."[16]

Why, then, had the Buddha been able (as had a few other innovators contemporary with him) to establish a powerful tradition in rejection of *śruti*? Without discounting his evidently powerful personality and the persuasiveness of his teaching, I think it is important to note that he had operated during a time of great social change in India, a time when many old certainties must have seemed shaken in the light of economic and political developments. He had spoken with confidence and an enormous fund of personal authority, and had managed to establish himself and his teaching as firm points in a drifting world. Thus, the Buddhist act of public commitment, to this day, entails the reciting of a formula by which the adept claims to "take refuge in the Buddha, the *dharma* and the *sangha*"—the great Founder, his teaching, and the institution he initiated. The idea of "taking refuge," of finding security in these, was evidently fundamental from the first.

By Gauḍapāda's time the authority of Buddhism had been strong and important for a millennium. It had sustained Indian hopes and guided many lives. But now it faced another of India's periodic moments of social crisis and, for many people, a corresponding weakening of confidence in stability and authority. A great Buddhist king, Harsha, was recently dead and his kingdom torn with dissent. A usurper, Arjuna, was defeated only by a combined Tibetan and Nepalese force and, as Vincent A. Smith puts it, "Harsha's death loosened the bonds which restrained the disruptive forces always ready to operate in India, and allowed them to produce their natural result, a medley of petty states, with ever-varying boundaries and engaged in unceasing internecine war."[17]

This is not to say that the period between Buddha and Gauḍapāda had been perfectly tranquil, but by Gauḍapāda's time Buddhism was old, sustained with solid scholarship and devotion, but among the lay masses, it perhaps lacked the vigor of its youth. When the new crisis came, it may well have seemed to some that a more ancient—even eternal—foundation was needed for human hope.

To grasp the seriousness of this—and Gauḍapāda's behavior—we may note that while Indian religious philosophy may resemble a centipede rather than a biped, it has had two particularly strong legs to stand on: a quest for irresistable authority and a quest for unfailing security. We shall elaborate this point briefly.

The 121st hymn of the 10th book of the *Ṛg Veda* seems to mark a decisive moment in Indian thought, although its date is impossible to determine. It is concerned largely with the origin of the world, and in each stanza it reiterates and intensifies a question about the ultimate source of things. Each of its verses, except the last (which may have been added by a later hand) ends with a common refrain: "Who is the God whom we should worship?" I do not think it stretches the flavor or intention of the hymn to see in this a question about supreme authority, for the God who is sought as the foundation of all that has come to exist must also be the source and guarantee of whatever value and meaning there can be in life, the authority for whatever can legitimately be pursued.

Whatever later scripture we turn to, and whatever form of deity is celebrated; whatever ritual cycle we examine, and whatever God is addressed, we can find this quest for or assertion of final authority always near the surface of Indian religious life and thought. Religion in India, then (as also elsewhere), is partly, but importantly, a matter of authority which endorses or establishes a trustworthy meaning and value for our living, and religious faith is not merely accepting some propositions as true, but a commitment, an investment of oneself in service to that authority. To lose confidence in an authority is, sooner or later, to withdraw that investment and to find in oneself a hunger for a new focus of value-endowing loyalty.

But that is not all. In the *Bṛhadāraṇyaka Upaniṣad* we learn that the primal being, Puruṣa, is alone in the universe. Indeed, it may be said that, at that moment, he *is* the universe. But he is afraid, and this puzzles him. He asks, very reasonably, "Of what am I fearful? There is nothing else!" With this realization the fear vanishes because, as the text clearly explains, "fear comes from another" (I.iv.2).

If the search for envaluing authority is one of the legs of Indian philosophy and religion, the longing for security and freedom from fear is another, and Puruṣa's solution will always remain strongly attractive: to eliminate fear by eliminating otherness. When I am aware of no "real" and irreducible "other" I am not aware of finitude and danger.

As we have noted, in its powerful era, Buddhism had presented the authority of a charismatic figure who had won a following even among the elite of his time, and whose tradition had then been given impetus by a great king, Aśoka, who had transformed what was formerly a local cult into a missionary tradition that showed promise of reaching the ends of the earth.

Strength had remained with Buddhism for centuries, but the retrospective eye can see, even before the beginning of the Common Era, the seeds of eventual weakness coming to fruition. The intrusion of more characteristic Hindu flavors of thought, the establishment of images and rituals in Buddhism's formerly largely iconoclastic style, the schismatic division of the *sangha* on matters of doctrine and practice, the endless debates, the failure to overcome social structures rooted in non-Buddhist sources—these and other factors grew more significant even as the Buddhist institution itself grew mature.

By Gauḍapāda's time Buddhism was still strong and may even be described as flourishing. Some of its finest exponents were at work and new schools emerged, seeming to indicate that its vigor was undiminished. Indeed, it would be further centuries before Buddhism disappeared from the Indian scene and, in the meantime, it would continue to offer security and the elimination of the risk-filled antithesis of self and other to many seekers. But the context in which Buddhism lived was changing. Political, economic and social forces were at work that may have been eroding some of the popular confidence in the Buddha's authority.

Perhaps we can see more clearly what had happened if we resort to a slightly modified version of Michel Foucault's thesis about power. Foucault asks us to consider the locus of power in society. He wishes to get beyond the typical debate between those who see power as possessed by particular agents and those who see it as produced by impersonal social structures. He recognizes that power is *exercised* by agents, but declines to think of these as *possessing* it. It is closer to the truth to say that an agent becomes the possibly fortuitous "place" where power is localized when the sweep of circumstance leads to such a possibility.

A society is a network of power relations, but a dynamic and changing one. Like a grammar, the "network" sets the limits of what may be "said" but does not absolutely determine it. Circumstances call forth new responses, and the power-network offers the limit but not the precise shape of the responses that may be made.[18]

In the evolving appreciation of what any generation considers to be "truth," then, dominant power systems are the source of constraints which lead to the approval of particular apprehensions, but if there is a shift in the shape of those power systems, the new configuration will make a new apprehension appear to be true.

What we are arguing is that at the time of the Buddha there was a change in the configuration of power that allowed several competing apprehensions to recommend themselves (the "heterodox" religious traditions that emerged then) and of these the Buddha's proved to be the strongest. By Gauḍapāda's time there had been an erosion of the power system that Buddhism had expressed and helped to form, however, and that permitted a new "truth" to be asserted compellingly. But the new truth consisted of a compromise between elements of Buddhism and the refurbished Vedic authority system whose roots were actually much older than Buddhism's.

To summarize, the common human desire for security was leading, in the slackening of Buddhism's authority because of the shift in social power-systems, to the construction of a new locus of authority, the recognition of a new "ground" of value whose explication might owe much to Buddhism, but whose rootage would need to be somewhere else. The Vedas, and especially the Upaniṣads, bound, as they were, to antiquity and entwined with powerful social forces and traditions, such as class and caste distinctions and functions, must have seemed a more enduring cradle of authority than the inspiration of the Buddha.

Gauḍapāda was a man of his age and reflects the residual strength of Buddhism as well as the renewed strength of the Upaniṣadic tradition. Thus he approved the ideas he had learned from Buddhism and the cultivated experience of non-duality they supported. But he wanted more assurance of authority to guarantee these values.

The solution was simple: ground the wisdom of the Buddha onto the authority of the Vedas. This was made easier because there was so much in the Upaniṣads that resembled Buddha's teaching anyway. It was not so difficult to color Upaniṣadic emphasis on the eternal, unique, unborn Brahman with the fully developed Mādhyamika notion that nothing was really produced; he could add resonances of Vijñānavāda's *citta-mātra* to the Upaniṣads' *ātman*. He could adapt Nāgārjuna's dialectic to the defense of a Vedāntic faith. He could, in short, have the advantages of highly developed Buddhist philosophy and experience, and of the *śrutī*'s mysterious and appealing authority.

In thus satisfying his own need, Gauḍapāda provided in Advaita Vedānta a means of settling the hearts of many others, to the present day. As T. M. P. Mahadevan has written, "Fear arises only when there is another. Where there is no other, fear cannot be. So Advaita is *abhaya*; non-duality is fearlessness. There is neither a *before* nor an *after* to the supreme Brahman. There is nothing different from it, and none whatever outside it."[19]

Perhaps the occasional passionate argument about Gauḍapāda's loyalty to Buddhism or Vedānta arises because he has become part of a system of meaning and authority that seems endangered by some speculation.

GROUNDS OF CONVICTION

Hindu philosophy has traditionally been careful to specify the *pramāṇas*, or means of knowledge, that it will accept as valid. This epistemological concern is, of course, important for any system of thought, especially for one that intends to argue for a particular appreciation of the world, and Gauḍapāda would have known half a dozen possible *pramāṇas* whose usefulness were claimed by various people. He seems to have chosen just three: reliance on scripture (or "verbal testimony"), reasoning (or "inference") and trust in experience, essentially sensory experience, but even and, in the end, especially the cultivated meditative experience of non-dual consciousness. Let us consider briefly the roles of these.

We have already suggested one reason for the appeal of *śruti* but we may now add more. T. M. P. Mahadevan suggests that *śruti*'s importance to religious philosophy arises from the recognition that reason itself is insufficient to reach understanding of the highest truths. He writes, "Thought must needs create division where there is unity in order that it may function." To clarify this, he adds: "It must distinguish; otherwise it will find its occupation gone. It cannot, therefore, be a competent instrument for the comprehension of the plenary reality which is distinctionless."[20]

All Hindu philosophical systems, whether non-dualist or not, accept the authority of *śruti* but Mahadevan shows us why the Advaitin's insistence that Reality is not truly divisible makes *śruti* an especially important addition to reason: if, like Guaḍapāda, one has the assumption that the final truth and reality must be utterly and indivisibly unmoving in its tranquil perfection, reason alone will, indeed, be unable to reach it.

We may make this point clearer if we oppose two possible visions of ultimacy. God is supremely perfect consciousness (where "perfect" means unchanging, unmoving); and God is supremely perfect reason (where "perfect" means dynamic, inventive, creative). If one begins with the first of these views, reason will deviate from the goal of describing or recognizing God; if one begins with the second, reason may achieve for us a sense of melting into an eternal creativity.

Gauḍapāda is a non-dualist of a very rigorous type, for whom the notion of even the slightest movement in Brahman, his ultimate, would have meant dualism. Therefore he needs a basis for conviction that defies reason and points to such absolute unity. Selected passages of the *śruti* provide what he wants.

But not all scriptures speak alike. How shall we deal, then, with those that suggest a more dualistic foundation of things? Why are they not to be preferred to the monistic ones?

The very instrument that proves unable to reach Brahman is now invoked to show that only the non-dualist scriptures are finally authoritative. In III.23 of his *kārikā* Gauḍapāda says that *śruti* is to be accepted only when it is compatible with reason! This use and support of reason is echoed elsewhere in the work (e.g., II.3, III.12, III.11, etc.) and he proceeds to make vigorous use of some of the modes of logic available to him, including the *reductio ad absurdum* argumentation of Hindu *tarka* and the dialectic of Nāgārjuna. What we are to see is that such weapons are used to discredit notions of duality, leaving the field open for the only alternative he knew: absolute non-duality. They could not reach a definition or description of the real, Brahman, but they could show what *śruti* was worthy of trust by demolishing the presupposition of the rest.

Śruti and reason are, therefore, an indispensible combination for Gauḍapāda, neither being quite sufficient without the other. Yet even together they are hardly enough. Indeed, even the addition of the third *pramāṇa* accepted by Gauḍapāda, perception (if understood simply as sensory experience) will not offer the certainty he seeks for his conviction of the immovability and oneness of Brahman, for Brahman is not to be perceived by the senses. If some *śruti* are shown to be mistaken, can one really be sure of the others? If reason has some limitation, can one be confident that it is a sufficiently sharp sword at any time? There is need of another ground of conviction, and Gauḍapāda found it in the immediate, meditatively stimulated experience of contentless consciousness which is *ātman* and, on the basis of scripture, may therefore be held to be Brahman.

Of what can we be certain? Never of an opinion, for fresh information may force us to change our mind. Never of empirical observation, for many things may distort this. But can we doubt that we are conscious?

Descartes' famous "*cogito ergo sum*" was an attempt to prove that "I" must exist because my thought certainly does. The more critical Vedāntist will not go so far. "I," the apparent thinker, may only be part of the thought itself! There may be only thinking!

But thinking is intermittent and changing. Is there a basis for it that is continous and unchanging? As we shall see, it seemed to Gauḍapāda that there was: a form of pristine consciousness that was the true ground on which all forms of thought rested, which pervaded them without itself being reduced to them. This was a "pure" awareness which content-awareness did not penetrate or pollute but without which no such defective awareness could exist.

To quote Mahadevan again, "It is consciousness *per se* which is the sole reality, according to Advaita." We obtain brief glimpses of it, he says, in "rare moments of introspection and exaltation," and "we pass into it in sleep." All these are very temporary experiences, however, and "to realize it in eternity is the aim of Vedānta."[21]

Here, then, we have the three bases on which Gauḍapāda (and Śaṅkara after him) founded their systems. All are important because mutually supportive. The experience of contentless, undivided consciousness might be no more than a function of the human organism, a mere electro-chemical event in the central nervous system, if there were not *śruti* to offer it a deeper meaning. *Śruti* would be a conflicting and confusing voice if reason did not show the invalidity of all but one of its perspectives. Reason is essentially divisive and could not bring us to the truth of Oneness if selected *śruti*, seemingly confirmed by contentless consciousness, did not point beyond it.

No one, or even two, of Gauḍapāda's *pramāṇas* would bring the certain assurance he sought. But the three together were, he believed, more sustaining even than the authority of the Buddha who had injudiciously dispensed with *śruti*.

MĀṆḌŪKYA UPANIṢAD AND GAUḌAPĀDA'S *KĀRIKĀS*

One of the delights in the study of ancient and complex documents is the unravelling of mysteries of lineage and relationship. In the case of Gauḍapāda's *kārikās* and the Upaniṣad to which we find them attached, several questions have exercised the patience and ingenuity of scholars. Among these the most persistent have been the exact nature of the relationship of *kārikās* to Upaniṣad, the status of this Upaniṣad among others of its class, and the relationship to each other of the four sections or chapters (*prakaraṇas*) of Gauḍapāda's work.

The Māṇḍūkya is a very short text, having only twelve verses. It is written in prose, and compresses its teaching so tightly that it is sometimes a little obscure. But the first real puzzle that scholars have had to try to solve arises from the fact that several old manuscripts combine the Upaniṣad and Gauḍapāda's first chapter, interweaving the contents of both. Thus the first six verses of the Upaniṣad are followed by nine verses of *kārikā*; the Upaniṣad's seventh verse is then followed by verses 10–18 of the *kārikā*; then come verses 8–11 of the Upaniṣad and 19–23 of the *kārikā* and, finally, verse 12 of the Upaniṣad and verses 24–29 of the *kārikā*.

What are we to make of this? Has Gauḍapāda, or some early editor, chosen to splice the two documents for the convenience of those who wish to use the *kārikās* to explicate the Upaniṣad? Perhaps, but there are alternative explanations.

Some have argued that this first chapter, or *prakaraṇa*, of the *kārikā* and the entire Upaniṣad are, and always were, a single work. Thus the followers of Madhva always treat them as if the entire set was the Upaniṣad and consider that Gauḍapāda's contribution does not begin until the second *prakaraṇa*. This seems unlikely, however, because of the difference in style between the two segments, a difference of which only the most conspicuous facet is that the "Upaniṣad" is prose and the "*kārikā*" poetry. Further, there are other manuscripts in which the Upaniṣad appears by itself—it is not consistently threaded by the *kārikā* passages. Above all, the distinction of Upaniṣad and *kārikā* and the attribution of only the latter to Gauḍapāda is at least as old as Śaṅkara.

Others have contended that the Upaniṣad and surrounding *kārikā* are, indeed, one work, but that all are by Gauḍapāda. This means that the Upaniṣad is not really *śruti* after all. There is some distinguished support for this view, including that of Max Walleser and Paul Deussen, and it has been defended recently by A. Venkatasubbiah who points out that the prose sections are very difficult to understand without the poetic *kārikās*. He reminds us that Śaṅkara, in his *bhāṣya* on the work, speaks of all four of the *prakaraṇas* as if he believed them to be a unified work, and since Gauḍapāda is known to have written most of them at least, Śaṅkara must have thought he wrote the Upaniṣad as well.[22]

Not everyone finds this persuasive, and Vidhushekhar Bhattacharya replies that there is really no solid reason for attributing the prose verses to Gauḍapāda. In fact, he says, not only did Gauḍapāda probably *not* write the prose (that is, the alleged Upaniṣad), but even the common view that his poetic verses were intended as commentary on the prose is false. How can one consider that the poetry is a commentary on the Upaniṣad when it fails to explain important terms and advances ideas that are not even mentioned in the *śruti* text?

But where does this leave us? Since the prose and poetry have been traditionally set in association for a very long time, surely they must have *some* legitimate connection! Yes, agrees Bhattacharya, but it is not that they share an author or that the Gauḍapādan verses interpret the Upaniṣad. On the contrary, what seems to be an Upaniṣad is actually an attempt by some unknown writer to summarize or condense the important elements in Gauḍapāda's work: it is the poetry, the *kārikā*, that came first![23]

Amar Nath Ray, among others, takes issue with Bhattacharya here. He points out that according to a tradition that cannot simply be ignored the Māṇḍūkya is one of the ten "major" Upaniṣads. Further, one near contemporary of Śaṅkara, Sureśvara, quoted from the Upaniṣad and actually named it, another, Māṇḍanomiśra, seems to be quoting from it, and Śaṅkara does the same in his *Bṛhadāraṇyaka Upaniṣad Bhāṣya*. Surely this proves that the Upaniṣad is older than the Gauḍapādan age and was regarded in that era as scripture. It could never have received, so early, this sort of attention if it had been written *after* Gauḍapāda's work.[24]

Raghunath Damodar Karmarkar offers yet another view. He agrees with Bhattacharya that the *kārikās* are not commentary on the Upaniṣad. They make no explicit claim to be a *bhāṣya*. Rather, they have a point of view to develop, but wish to show that it is soundly consistent with *śruti*, so a congenial Upaniṣad was selected and then those of its ideas that were found to be pertinent were creatively—and selectively! discussed.[25]

It is probably impossible to reach a confident conclusion on this subject, or at least a conclusion that will compel assent. The traditional view—that Gauḍapāda wrote the first *prakaraṇa* of the whole *kārikā* on the basis of an established Upaniṣad— seems at least as sound as any. In any case, since we are concerned with Gauḍapāda's system of ideas, the relation of Upaniṣad and *kārikās* need detain us no longer.

Of more concern is another question: are the four *prakaraṇas* or chapters of Gauḍapāda's book really intended to belong together, or are they a set of independent essays that happen somehow to have been put together arbitrarily?

It has often been pointed out that it is quite possible to take any one of these sections and treat it as a self-contained work. The first deals selectively with the Upaniṣad in some fashion and, in doing so, explains that reality is non-dual; it uses the idea of dreamless sleep to suggest the character of this reality. The second argues that objects seen when we are fully awake are as illusory as those known in dreams, and goes on to argue that the supreme *ātman* is not only "real" but is unchanging and eternal. The third defends the notion of non-duality against various possible assaults, and the fourth then leads us through many of the points previously made, but does so in a systematic manner, drawing heavily on Buddhist terminology.

While it is quite possible to make a case for the original independence of all the *prakaraṇas*, there is a commonality of style and a continuity of thought in the first three that lends support to the conventional opinion that they belong together. The fourth, however, has unique features, and even those who prefer to believe that all four constituted a single work from the beginning are often inclined to concede that the last *may* have begun its career separately. It is interesting, although hardly decisive, to note in defence of the independence of the final *prakaraṇa* that the third concludes on the kind of epigrammatic note that might well signal the end of a study, and the fourth begins with an invocation that sounds like the beginning of one. Further, the fact that the fourth is comprised of a neat one hundred verses lends a little weight to the suggestion that it was meant to be whole and independent.

Whether the fourth *prakaraṇa* was or was not, at first, a new and separate effort, it is sufficiently self-contained to justify our treating it as a brief compendium of Gauḍapāda's philosophy, and this is what the main body of this work will do.

Gauḍapāda's *kārikās*, then, begin with reference to an Upaniṣad, and we may infer that this was chosen because it was congenial (more, perhaps, than most) to Gauḍapāda's position. It may be worth noting that while Vedāntists prize it highly, considering it among the ten major works of its kind, and a brave soul has sometimes said that it is of early date, the linguistic evidence suggests strongly that it is among the later Upaniṣads, and may well itself have enjoyed (or suffered) Buddhist influence. This is Caterina Conio's opinion, and she defends it by pointing out that the *Māṇḍūkya* contains words like *prapañca upaśama* (in verse 7) "which do not belong to the language of classical Upaniṣad, but seem to belong to a post Nāgārjuna period."[26]

The fourth *prakaraṇa* is the one that shall concern us. But it may not be quite useless to outline the contents of the other three. We shall draw upon them, from time to time, to clarify issues that arise in the fourth.

SUMMARIES OF *PRAKARAṆAS* I, II, AND III

PRAKARAṆA I: "ĀGAMA"

The *Māṇḍūkya Upaniṣad* declares that the mystic syllable "*Om*" is Brahman, the final reality itself. It was not an uncommon idea in the ancient world to identify certain entities with a sound that represented them. This is why, in some societies, names of persons were so "sacred" that they might not be freely shared with all others; the name was not simply a label, but in a mysterious way was the person her or himself, or at least participated in the person's reality.

But the Upaniṣad breaks down "*Om*" into constituent parts, and identifies each part with one experience of human consciousness: "*A*" is our waking state, "*U*" is our dreaming, "*M*" is dreamless sleep, and all together "*Aum*" or "*Om*" stands for a fourth form of consciousness (*Turya*) which comprehends all the others as their root and reality. (In pursuit of euphony, Sanskrit converts a juxtaposed "A" and "U" to "O.")

One implication is clear, and lies near the center of Gauḍapāda's system: our reality—indeed *all* reality—is consciousness, and consciousness undergoes modifications but is always, at root, the same.

Gauḍapāda wishes to press the images of the Upaniṣad further, ensuring our close identification with the elements of "*Om*." So he says that the first three of these sounds and states of consciousness are each focussed in a particular feature of the human body. *M*" represents *prajñā* (intelligence, understanding; here probably meaning the basic consciousness of the individual). This is identified with the heart or heart-space. "*U*" is dreaming, and is focussed in the mind. "*A*" is wakefulness and is associated with the right eye.

The location of "*A*" certainly seems strange, and Indian commentators have struggled with it. Perhaps the right eye was thought by Gauḍapāda to be naturally the stronger of the two, and vision was believed by him to be the highest feature of wakefulness. Anyway, the point is that all that we are is somehow to be identified with modifications of consciousness.

Now, this analysis is extended in Gauḍapāda's thought to all things: *there is no objectivity outside consciousness.*

If this is true, why is there a world? And what can be the nature of that troublesome world?

Gauḍapāda alludes to prevailing theories: the world is the expression of God's will; it is a product of Time; it is for God's sport; it is God's nature to create, and so on. All these explanations are rejected. He points out that the highest reality, or God, is known as *Āptakāma*, the one whose desires are fulfilled, and if this is true, how could that reality create anything? No one who is perfectly satisfied does anything. The idea that a Being might be so rich in perfection that he/she/it created out of its superabundant fullness belongs to Judaic, Christian or Muslim thought.

These abandoned theories all take the material world as real, and once one has identified the supreme reality as a perfect *consciousness* the possibility that this could give rise to genuine *matter* seems remote. At best it might entertain the *idea* of a material world. And even such an idea could have no importance or "truth" for a consciousness that was perfect.

The world, then, must be regarded as *māyā*, illusion. The perfect One is all the reality there is, and the appearance of any other, of duality, is necessarily false, although we (who, as seemingly solid individuals, are part of the falsehood) take it seriously because of our ignorance (*avidyā*). The sixteenth verse then promises that "when the individual spirit, which has been asleep because of beginningless *māyā*, wakes up, it realizes the Non-dual which is unborn, sleepless and dreamless."

We may summarize Gauḍapāda's views in this *prakaraṇa* as follows: dreamless sleep is non-apprehension, but *Turya*, perfectly contentless consciousness, is reality itself, and when it is experienced, duality disappears. There is no longer a knowing self, a known object, or a condition of objective knowing. The path to this happy realization is meditation on "*Om*."

PRAKARAṆA II: "VAITHATHYA"

The reader should be warned that, in the pursuit of clarity, we shall use images and metaphors that are not in Gauḍapāda's text. This is not a translation but a summary and explanation of the main ideas in the text.

Śaṅkara, in his commentary[27], tied this *prakaraṇa* to the last by saying that Gauḍapāda here uses reason to develop and defend what the previous section taught simply on the basis of scripture. This is largely plausible, for the main point of the present section is to show that all apparent entities are really modes of consciousness and that those we encounter in the condition of wakefulness are no more "real" (or material) than those of our dreams. Śaṅkara was later to modify this a little, wanting to preserve some distinction between dream and waking perceptions and to allow the latter a higher measure of relative value, but in the end it is true, even for him, that consciousness is Brahman and is undividedly all there is.

First, we must agree that images seen in dreams are pure imagination. If we dream of a mountain, we know, as soon as we awaken, that there was no real mountain because the dream happened inside our head and there is no room there for a thing as large as a mountain. Nor can we imagine that we actually visited such a thing while asleep, because we find ourselves exactly where we were when we fell asleep and there has usually not been time for us to travel to the mountain and back.

What is not so obvious is that the images of our wakeful experience are just as insubstantial. But, in fact, they are as surely discredited by our dreaming as our dreaming is by our waking. If we eat a full meal, go to sleep, and then dream of being hungry, is not the actuality of the meal just as completely falsified as if we had dreamed of it and awakened to hunger? Any state that is temporary is less than real, so dreaming disconfirms wakeful experience as much as the latter disconfirms our dreams.

The unstated premise behind this argument was an old dictum that anything that is not real at some time, or comes to be no longer real at another time, cannot have been real at any time. In other words, whatever is real is always present because it cannot cease to be, and whatever is not present does not exist, and cannot begin to exist because there is nothing that can come to existence out of nothing.

Perhaps we should note that this argument is just a little dangerous because it can be twisted. That is, instead of saying, as Gauḍapāda does, that the dream-object formerly did not exist, then seemed to exist, and then no longer existed and therefore cannot ever have been real, one might say that since the object *did* exist at some time, and whatever *is* cannot cease to be, it must have existed always and must exist still: its disappearance, therefore, is illusion!

At this point Gauḍapāda responds to an objection that he has evidently heard or anticipates. One might say, Ah, but the things I dream about are not actually useful, while the things I know when awake are. This is a sort of pragmatic test: can you cut a "real" cake with a dream knife? No. But you *can* cut it with the knife you hold when awake. It is the fulfilment of some purpose with an object that demonstrates its reality.

Not so, says Gauḍapāda. I can cut a dream cake with a dream knife just as surely as I can cut a "waking" cake with my "waking" knife, and the waking knife vanishes in my dream as my dream knife disappears when I awake. Both are equally temporary and therefore equally false.

But, protests the objector, dream images are often fantastic, bizarre. That surely shows that they are of a different character than the sober objects of my waking state.

No; even if it is true that the images seen when awake are less elaborate and fanciful than those in dreams, they are just as surely temporary since we do not remain eternally aware of them, and therefore they are just as false.

Here the objector is troubled by a sudden and important bewilderment. If all our experience is an illusion, including our experience of ourselves as independent individuals, who is having the illusion, and how does it arise?

Gauḍapāda replies that the self-luminous *Ātman* brings forth the illusion by its own power. Nothing whatever really comes into existence: *Ātman*, the supreme Brahman, is the cause of the entire array of fantasy. It "imagines itself by its own power" says verse 12, implying that the ultimate and singular *Ātman* both creates and experiences the illusion.

This is a daring proposition that Śaṅkara had to abandon, probably because if this is true it would seem either that the *Ātman* (Brahman) is self-deceived and therefore imperfect, or it takes pleasure in its creative imagination—and in Vedāntic terms this also would mean that it had needs to satisfy and was imperfect.

Gauḍapāda does not seem to recognize this problem, and pursues his theme. He outlines a number of theories about the status of things and although he does not pause to discredit them with argument, he counters them with his non-dualistic hypothesis that the whole mass of existents is no more than imagination in *Ātman*.

In verse 32 he gives us a conclusion that is strikingly similar to verses in the Buddhist *Laṅkāvatāra Sūtra*.[28] There is, he says, neither an end nor a beginning, neither anyone in bondage to ignorance nor anyone seeking wisdom; there is no one actually striving for liberation and no one actually liberated. In a word, there are *no* particular existents. This, he says, is the supreme truth.

Even the idea of non-duality is less than absolute truth, precisely because it is an *idea*. The non-dual itself, shining without the least vestige of duality, is not fragmented even by ideas.

This means that the person who has awakened to the truth is that truth itself, and no longer has any use for rituals, for ordinary responsibilities, or for a home. He carries on whatever must be done in the world as if he were an insensate object (verse 36).

PRAKARAṆA III: "ADVAITA"

This chapter is devoted to argument in favor of the absolute truth of monism: all is one.

Obviously monism, or non-dualism, as a theory conflicts rather dramatically with our everyday experience of the world. There are things and persons that certainly seem to be as real as we ourselves are, and yet quite "other" than we. If all is one, how can this be?

Gauḍapāda resorts to a metaphor to answer our question. Consider space (actually he uses *ākāśa* which properly means something more like the old English term "ether," a universally pervasive air-like stuff, but space will do as well). When Brahman appears as individual persons (*jīvas*) it is like space appearing within jars. When a jar is smashed, the space within it becomes again indistinguishable from space in general because it never really was other. Similarly when the individual dissolves in enlightenment, the *Ātman* that was his or her reality is found not to be different from the universal Brahman. (We may note in passing that this does not account for the jar or show that *it* is not quite as real as the space. But metaphors should never be pushed too far—or relied on as argument.)

Further, when a pot is tarnished or marked by dirt, nothing occurs to the space within. Nor do other pots receive the same mark. So individuals seem to suffer their own pains and joys, but *Ātman* is not touched and since *Ātman* is all, the individuality of experience is illusion.

But, says an objector, are there not respectable scriptures which speak as if individuality were real? Yes, answers Gauḍapāda, but they are speaking expediently, not quite truly. The sad fact is that not everyone is intellectually ready for the pure truth of Advaita, so some scriptures generously address them with a level of understanding (which is also necessarily a level of misunderstanding) that they can grasp. This will be of help to them, but it must not be mistaken for absolute truth.

The truth really is that the immortal can never become mortal, nor the mortal become immortal, for nothing can ever change its character: what is must always be as it is. If we said that something has been produced, this would mean that it had formerly been unproduced. But for the unproduced to be produced is for it to change its character, to become something it never was, and this is absurd.

Therefore nothing is ever produced, and the appearance of change, growth, beginnings and endings, is nothing more than *māyā*, illusion. Our dreaming or waking visions are mere vibrations of our mind, and when in deep, dreamless sleep the mind ceases to vibrate, the visions also cease. But this is only a temporary release, and final emancipation from illusion cannot come to us until the mind achieves a complete stillness in *samādhi*.

Samādhi is derived from a root, "*dhī*" which means mind or intellect, and with the addition of "*sam*" and "*a*" becomes "comprehensive" intellect. It is the condition achieved in deep meditation when the flow of thought has been suspended and all sensations, ideas, and images are obliterated. For the procedure that leads to this Gauḍapāda now introduces the term *asparśayoga*, which literally means the "touchless" yoga, the yoga that leads us to the state where our consciousness is so withdrawn, so introverted, that it loses touch with all objects, including ideas. This is the moment when the mind ceases to vibrate and we discover the changeless, birthless *Atman*.

"*Asparśayoga*" is certainly not a word used in the authoritative literature of Vedānta before Gauḍapāda, but it does occur in Buddhist writing, and we see here evidence of the influence of that tradition. This becomes far more marked in the fourth and final *prakaraṇa*.

Gauḍapāda warns his readers, however, that to embark on the *samādhi* path is not to be beyond the danger of seduction. One of the side-effects of meditative accomplishment can be, and usually is, a certain happiness and satisfaction. This must be firmly set aside. Meditation, for Gauḍapāda, is decidedly not for the sake of pleasure but for the transcending of all sensation and emotion.

Gauḍapāda ends this section with a reiteration of his central conviction: "No entity whatever is born; there is never any origination of anything. This is the supreme truth: *nothing whatever comes into existence*" (verse 48).

Critics have occasionally noted what may seem to be an awkward inconsistency in this section. If the individual *jīva* or person is an imagination of the supreme *Ātman*, but the continuation of the *jīva's* existence is to be repudiated and undone, are we not implying a criticism of the *Ātman*? It is almost as though, discontented with the Brahman's achievement, we are trying to correct it. If it is better for Brahman to be without the imagination of a world, is Brahman not inept or unwise to imagine one? And if our work to achieve contentless consciousness is, after all, Brahman's own work, then Brahman is active and this means less than tranquilly perfect; if, on the other hand, it is *not* Brahman's own work, then we who do it seem to have a measure of separate reality that the theory disavows. The usual response to such objections is that they arise from the dualizing intellect and are therefore irrelevant; put it to rest and the problems disappear.

PRINCIPAL IDEAS IN THE FOURTH *PRAKARAṆA*: "ĀLĀTAŚANTI"

A feature of this *prakaraṇa* is the series of arguments employed to prove the non-dualist position. We shall leave the analysis of these until the next section, however, and be content herein to summarize the main ideas that are developed or, more often, simply affirmed. There are actually very few of these, but they constitute the basis on which the long and living tradition of Advaita Vedānta has been built. It will quickly become obvious that most of the ideas we are about to meet have already appeared in the earlier *prakaraṇas*.

The first important premise we shall find offered is that all objects of awareness, all the things of the experienced world, are really insubstantial and even false. Reality is not a complex of various things, or even a partnership of two. It is one.

To convince us of this, Gauḍapāda reminds us of the states of consciousness that are common: waking, dreaming, and dreamless sleep. It is an assumption of common sense that objects seen in sleep are only mental fabrications, while those perceived while we are awake are "real." Gauḍapāda challenges this.

Why do we think that objects seen when we are awake are more real than those we dream about? Surely not because they are more enduring! When we turn our attention from them we soon forget them; they disappear as completely as the dream. Clearly, then, they belong to the imagination just as the dream does.

Nor are objects of our wakeful consciousness really more practical and useful than dreams. Dream water quenches dream thirst as effectively as the water of wakeful experience quenches wakeful thirst.

The critical point to remember is that the objects of wakeful experience are as fully obliterated from consciousness in sleep as dream objects are when we awake. In technical terms, each set of "objects" is sublated in turn by the other, so why would we suppose that one sort of object is more substantial or superior to the other?

An axiom of Advaitic philosophy is that whatever is real remains so without change; whatever is, at any moment, unreal can never become real. The real is only whatever is always, changelessly present. But objects of both waking and dreaming are all present only while we are conscious of them, so they must depend on our consciousness and what is dependent for its existence cannot be said to be real in any final sense. The waking world is like the dreamed one: they are "real" in exactly the same sense and measure.

But if objects of consciousness are thus less than perfectly real in an independent sense, surely this is true of consciousness itself. Objects are only states of consciousness and are shown to be non-real because they are transient; but this means that consciousness itself is a sequence of transient states and must, therefore, finally be transient (that is, unreal) itself. Is there anything that has the qualities of permanence, stability, and changelessness that alone qualify anything to be called "real"?

When we sleep, our dreaming is punctuated by times of pure mental quiescence—deep dreamlessness. But this is not to be thought of as an absense of consciousness for, if it were, consciousness could never return (on the premise, already stated, that what does not at any time exist cannot begin to do so). Consciousness of objects *does* return, and this proves that some mode of consciousness, the permanent substratum of all others, was present all the time. This mode of consciousness, this "consciousness in-itself" or pure consciousness must be, then, more enduring than any content or shape it might assume, and must be present even as the basis of dreamless sleep.

This ultimate consciousness is the support and reality of all the familiar conditions of mind, waking, dreaming, and dreamlessness; it is *Turya*, the fourth mode which is, at the same time, the only thing that is eternal, changeless and utterly real. Andrew O. Fort has well summarized the point thus: "The flux of everyday states of consciousness (like waking, dream, and deep sleep) is said to point to the advaitin's basic philosophical conviction, that there is a single, eternally self-luminous substratum of existence (*ātman/brahman*)."[29]

Turya, then, is pure consciousness. It comes to be overlaid by images in dream and waking, and it is closest to its perfection, so far as our common experiences are concerned, during dreamless sleep. It knows no boundaries, for there is in it no object to provide a limit, and it is untouched by time. This is *ātman*. In verse 45 we find the familiar Vijñānavāda term *vijñāna* used as Gauḍapāda sums up the position: "What appear to be origination, movement, and things are really the unborn, unmoving, substanceless consciousness, peaceful and non-dual."

It should be noted that Theravāda Buddhists had, long ago, argued that there is no such substratum-consciousness, that consciousness is a series of momentary entities, not an unbroken continuum, and while Gauḍapāda obviously finds this unacceptable, he does not directly confront the essential question asked by the Theravādins: *why* must there be an eternal substratum to sustain a sequence of temporary things? Where Gauḍapāda would doubtless have found the idea of sequence without an unchanging basis unimaginable because if no entity were permanent there could not be anything at all, the Theravādins thought that an experienced sequence that was inherently beginningless and endless was more easily conceivable than a permanent and unchanging something that no living, empirical person had ever experienced permanently and unchangingly!

Ignoring the Theravādins, then, Gauḍapāda offers us

his first major idea: plurality is less than real, and what *is* real is single, unchanging, eternal, and is contentless consciousness.

This means that materiality is imaginary; that *stasis* is the character of reality, not process; that "being" is eternal and there is no "becoming." As in an earlier *prakaraṇa*, Gauḍapāda finds it necessary now to say something about the nature of the world we seem to experience, a world that is utterly different from his notion of what is real, for it is a process that never stops its movement, it is a complex of many particular things rather than a single one, and it is material enough to break our bones if we fall on it.

Is there a world because God makes one? Popular religion may say so, and even Gauḍapāda may have an occasional phrase that seems to suggest something like it, but on his premisses this cannot be the truth. The highest reality (the *only* reality, in the final resort) is Brahman (which is also to be known as *Ātman*, the eternal spirit) and since this is unchanging, unmoving, at perfect rest, wanting nothing, it can be neither the efficient cause nor the material cause of a world. Later Advaitins, including Śaṅkara, will sometimes suggest that Brahman is the material cause of things (*upādāna-kāraṇa*), but this cannot really be the case, for Brahman would then have undergone some kind of modification or change. And certainly it cannot be the efficient cause of things, for that would mean that it had moved, acted, and demonstrated a need to be creative.

No, on Gauḍapāda's premises no God, and certainly not Brahman without whose effort no lesser god could exist, has created the world.

Is the world, then, itself eternal, like Brahman? No, for its members have been shown to be no more real than dreams. Further, if it were real, Brahman would be limited by that which is not Brahman, and this is unthinkable.

So with Brahman the sole reality, too perfect to create anything or to undergo any change, the things of everyday experience must be no things at all: *ajāti*— unborn, unproduced, uncreated, unarising; in a word, unreal.

But we see them! Then what we see is like a mirage, a dream, a fantasy. But we who dream are no more real than our images, for if we were we, too, would limit Brahman. We, then, and what we experience or perceive alike are *māyā*, illusion. As we are told in verse 71: "No individual entity is born: no such beginning ever takes place. This is the ultimate truth: nothing whatever is originated!"

In our next section we shall examine more closely the arguments offered to support this idea of non-origination, but let us first take note of some other important ideas, beginning with that of *māyā* itself.

As we saw when discussing Gauḍapāda's sources, the term *māyā* underwent changes of meaning during the long period between the *Ṛg Veda* and Gauḍapāda. Grammarians have sometimes derived the word from a root, *mā*, which means either to measure or to show. Advaitins have liked this because it suggests that *māyā* is a mere "show" by which the immeasurable Brahman *seems* to be reduced to measurable things. It is certainly in the sense of deception, illusion, falsity that Gauḍapāda uses the term.

So the things of the world are mere show and do not really affect the immeasurable itself. The moon I "see" and the apple I "eat" are no more substantial than those I dream.

But then we are bound to ask, who is imagining the products of *māyā*? Not this individual, for this individual is himself a piece of the *māyā*. It is in response to this that Gauḍapāda ventures an opinion so fraught with problems that Śaṅkara, and most later Advaitins, have had to reject his suggestion, although one can say that their alternatives have not been much more successful in avoiding one of the thorniest problems of non-dualist philosophy.

In outlining Gauḍapāda's second *prakaraṇa* we drew attention to Gauḍapāda's attempt to deal with the problem, but we should spend a little more time on it now. In II.12 he says that *Ātman*, meaning the supreme, solitary Brahman, is one who "imagines" itself by means of its own *māyā*. This idea is repeated in verse 19 of the same *prakaraṇa*. This seems to mean that Brahman projects an image of itself, an illusion of itself in the multiform shapes of the universe. But this will hardly do! It would imply either that Brahman chooses to dream its dream (in which case the dream is purposeful and Brahman is not so "perfect" as had been claimed), or, if Brahman does not *choose*, then it is the involuntary victim of illusion—surely an even less happy situation, since a victimized Brahman must mean a state of helplessness also for those who trust it as the answer to their suffering.

Some readers have seen in Gauḍapāda the shadow of a theory that reached its fullest development a little later. According to this, Brahman-in-itself is *nirguṇa*, without qualities or limitations of any kind; but people who seek an explanation of the world may be led to impose certain qualities on Brahman, such as creativity, love, purposiveness, and so on. When they do, they derive a notion which can be called *saguṇa*-Brahman, or Brahman modified by qualities. This qualified Brahman is what theists mean by "God," but for Advaitins it is merely a concept, a mental fiction, for in truth Brahman has no such limiting qualities.

On this theory, Gauḍapāda is saying that while *nirguṇa*-Brahman contemplates no world, *saguṇa*-Brahman imagines one creatively. Obviously this solves nothing. To say that the devotee who worships God has imposed imaginary features on Brahman is one thing; to say that Brahman imagines itself as having qualities is another, and if Brahman is the efficient cause of *māyā* or, through *māyā*, of the world-effect, then this is what is meant.

Is it possible that we have here a point at which Gauḍapāda is tripped up by his attempt to weld the viewpoint of Vijñānavāda Buddhism to Advaita Vedānta? In the former, the supreme *Vijñāna* is assumed to be perfect in itself but, in a sense, dynamic (rather than static, like Brahman). It is stable and always self-consistent, yet it contains the process by which a continuous flow of ideas is brought to fruition by *karma*. It is *dhruva*, enduring, but not in all respects *nitya*, unchanging, for it contains or supports the process of *māyā* (in the *mano-vijñāna*) without being actually corrupted. The *alayavijñāna*, that is, of Vijñānavāda, although similar in many ways, is fundamentally different from the Brahman-*Ātman* of Vedānta. It satisfies the need to account for a ground of process but does so by failing to be quite perfectly static and "solid." Brahman *is* unmoving in all respects, but thus fails to provide a ground for process. Gauḍapāda may have the unenviable task of trying to yoke two mutually incompatible horses in an attempt to enjoy what he sees as the benefits of each.

But perhaps we should concede that Gauḍapāda at least recognized his dilemma. In verse 52 he says of our mental impressions and images, "They are always incomprehensible."

Further, the consolation offered us is that the problem remains only so long as mental activity remains, and when Brahman is perfectly realized, this comes to an end, bringing *māyā* to oblivion with it: "ce mot [*māyā*] connote l'erreur qui n'existe qu'autant que la vérité se trouve méconnue, mais s'évanouit devant la vérité acquise."[30]

That nothing whatever is born, produced, created or otherwise initiated is, then, Gauḍapāda's foremost suggestion. That all that we sense, and we the sensors, are *māyā*, illusion, is his second. There are several subsidiary notions that we may very briefly mention.

As William M. Indich points out, until Aurobindo, Vedāntic philosophers have tended to think very statically about the different kinds or levels of consciousness.[31] One did not merge into another: it was "sublated." This is true also of Mahāyana Buddhists in general, at least until they came under Chinese influence. Gauḍapāda is an example of this tendency, and we find that the pure consciousness that is *Ātman* is "real," while all other forms of awareness are, by contrast, less than real. Śaṅkara modified this disjunction to the extent that he allowed variable value to waking perceptions, dreams, and delusions, but even for him all these were radically separated from enlightenment. Indich correctly observes that Vedāntins are traditionally given to the use of *sthana* for "state" of consciousness, a word derived from the root *stha* which means to stand, remain, or rest.

Between *Turya*, perfect consciousness (which is Brahman) and *māyic* forms of perception, then, there is a gulf. With a similar understanding, Nāgārjuna had taught that there are two levels of discourse, and no one can understand the Buddha's teaching unless he or she first grasps this fact. There is teaching that is effective within the sphere of illusion, and teaching that belongs to that of enlightenment, and if one takes the former as if it were the latter (if, that is, one takes something offered as a concession to our blindness and uses it as if it were absolute truth) one misses the Buddha's point entirely.

Thus, a sentence that makes good, practical sense in the realm of ordinary experience is *samvṛti-satya*, or relative truth, while the absolute truth is *paramārtha-satya*.

Strictly speaking, the absolute truth must be wordless: it is beyond the sort of experience out of which language is created, and Nāgārjuna and his followers made much of the silence with which the Buddha responded to certain questions. This silence was not, they said, a refusal to answer but the correct answer: it was the acknowledgment that *samvṛti-satya* owns all the words and *paramārtha-satya* is free (or "empty," *śūnya*) of them all.

Despite this separation of the verbal relative and the supra-verbal absolute, words can and must be used to awaken sensitivity to the possibility of enlightenment. It is, however, a unique language game that the enlightened play when they torture ordinary terms to point beyond ordinary experience.

In later Vedānta we find the development of this idea of levels of discourse or of truth, and it becomes important as early as Śaṅkara. Gauḍapāda cannot be said to have been very explicit about it, but he does set the stage when, in IV.42 he tells us: "The Enlightened One teaches things about 'origination' for the sake of realists who are persuaded by their ordinary experience, by conventional opinion, and by their fear of the idea that there is no origination of anything."

This verse reminds us of Nāgārjuna, but its importance is that it justifies the development of a system of philosophy while leaving open the possibility of tactical retreat from that system into wordlessness when this seems the safer course. It is difficult to defeat in debate a philosopher who will pursue vigorously his or her line of reason while it is successful, and light-heartedly step away from it when it fails!

Reason and language, then, are strictly instrumental and limited for Gauḍapāda's successors, and he has himself laid the foundation for this development by borrowing from Nāgārjuna the idea that even the enlightened may say things that are not absolutely true, but are relatively useful.

Since Brahman is beyond words, the most important avenue of approach (in the end, the only effective one) is not philosophy but meditative discipline, the manipulation of consciousness to lead it into conformity with what one has come to believe about Brahman. This discipline is given a name by Gauḍapāda that is not drawn from the Upaniṣadic tradition. He calls it *Asparśayoga*.

"*Asparśa*" means without contact, touchless, and in the present context it signifies a form of consciousness that is completely bereft of sensation or even of ideas and mental operations. It is a stillness which, while not mere *unconsciousness*, is free of objects, free of content.

Such unblinking, bare consciousness is the goal for an Advaitin, because so long as there is even a single image in the mind, we are experiencing duality—thinker and thought. Only when the thinker is unaware of thought, even the thought that thinking is happening, is pure non-duality achieved. Brahman, being quite free of duality, cannot even be aware of itself, for that would make it an object for its consciousness and duality would be born. It is simple, pure, undivided awareness, and nothing more. To say that it is "bliss" (*ānanda*), therefore, does not mean it has *sensations* of bliss, that it actively enjoys happiness: rather, it means that bliss in this Vedāntic tradition is absolute peace, and even that "peace" must be understood to be no emotion but freedom from emotion.

In the present *prakaraṇa* Gauḍapāda does not tell us much about his yoga, but verse 90 offers something. The "Agrayāṇa" is mentioned as a source of guidance, but this has aroused some controversy because the term is held by some to refer directly to Buddhism and by others merely to the ancient axioms of the spiritual life. In any case, from the Agrayāṇa we are supposed to learn what ought to be realized, what appropriated, what rendered unproductive, and what avoided. Since Gauḍapāda does not enlarge on these categories, except to say that apart from "what should be realized" they all refer to items of ordinary experience, we must depend on the commentators.

That which is to be realized is obviously the non-dual *ātman* itself; that which we must appropriate, according to Śaṅkara, is the proper method of meditative discipline; passions of every sort are what we must render unproductive, and it is empirical experience that must be avoided—our meditation must drive out all "touch" with the world.

Asparśayoga is, thus, a mental discipline that expunges from consciousness all content. But not everyone is ready or equipped to plunge directly into such perfect introversion, so more guidance is needed. For this we must turn back to the first *prakaraṇa* where Gauḍapāda deals with the *Māṇḍūkya Upaniṣad.*

As we have seen, this Upaniṣad presents the sacred syllable "*Om*" as the focus of effective meditation, and its analysis of the elements of this sound guide the enquirer into a deepened grasp of what consciousness is, what its various levels are, and what perfect consciousness would be. Gauḍapāda promises, in IV.89, that when the three common kinds of consciousness are "understood in the correct order, omniscience spontaneously awakens in a person of great intellect."

The goal of all Hindu systems of religion is *mokṣa*, liberation. Let us, finally, ask what Gauḍapāda has to say about this.

We must be prepared for the fact that *mokṣa*, being outside the range of ordinary experience, is also beyond the reach of ordinary language. Much that is said of it is therefore negative: it is easier to say what *mokṣa* is not than to say what it is. Thus in the fourth *prakaraṇa* we find that it is not sorrow or fear or desire (verse 78), that it is not action (80), that it has no plurality (100), that it lacks any differences or distinctions (95), and even when seemingly positive terms are used, they must be understood as not bearing quite their usual denotation or connotation. So when we read that *mokṣa* entails omniscience (89) we should not imagine that this implies that the fully liberated person knows everything (literally every *thing* or fact) but that his "knowing" is whole and undivided—which, in fact, means contentless. Again, when peace (*śānti*) is used to describe *mokṣa*, it means the complete absense of disturbance including those disturbances that are usually considered beneficent, such as elation or happiness.

In Buddhism the root trouble of human life is *duḥkha*, pain, anxiety, diminishment, sorrow, suffering. The end of *duḥkha* is therefore *nirvāṇa* (a term, incidentally, that Gauḍapāda is prepared to use) and this literally means extinguishing, but should probably be more aptly rendered in the Buddhist context as ceasing to acquire things, concepts, attitudes, experiences, and, above all, *karma*. The Mādhyamikan saw that to realize what we really are is to know ourselves as *śūnya*, indeterminate, without characteristics, *karma*, or *kleśa* (passion). The Vedāntist avoids the term *śūnya*, but declares that our reality is nothing other than Brahman (*tat tvam asi*: "That thou art," or *aham Brahma asmi*: "I am Brahman") and this, no less than Mādhyamika's *śūnyatā* means to be quite indeterminate.

Mokṣa, then, is the experience of indeterminacy. How may one continue to live in the world after *mokṣa* is realized? One must simply flow with the necessities of circumstance, egolessly doing what falls to one's lot. As Gauḍapāda says in II.36, such a liberated person goes on with actions as if insensate. To the worldling this may not sound attractive, but it is certainly peaceful.

Here we end our outline of the content of our text. It remains for us only to restate in convenient language the essence of the arguments which Gauḍapāda uses to prove his basic point: that there is no production or arising of any real entities.

ARGUMENTS FOR *AJĀTI* (NON-PRODUCTION)

Although our text is replete with partial reiterations, the arguments for the doctrine that nothing real comes into existence can be conveniently summarized. The main body of these arguments is concerned with proving that causal relationship does not actually obtain anywhere, and while Gauḍapāda does not write with the precision and order that a logician might desire, we can assemble his premisses.

He is clearly dependent on the critical dialectic of Nāgārjuna, who was intent to show that only four possible relations can exist between cause and effect, and that to propose any of them leads inevitably into contradiction. For Nāgārjuna this simply ruled out thought as an effective instrument; for Gauḍapāda it eliminates the reality of anything except Brahman. To grasp Gauḍapāda's reasoning we have to allow him a presupposition that was probably founded on his own meditative experience of non-dual, contentless consciousness, a condition that he identified with Brahman. Brahman, thus, was not a debatable entity. It is motionless, purposeless, passionless, tranquil, indivisible and eternal. Grant him this, and he will try to show that nothing else is possible at all.

For Nāgārjuna, the four possible relations of cause and effect were the following:

1. Cause is different from Effect.
2. Cause is identical with Effect.
3. Cause and Effect are different *and* identical.
4. Cause and Effect are *neither* different nor identical.

We shall gather Gauḍapāda's scattered arguments under these four headings, indicating the source, within the text, of each by a verse number in parenthesis after our restatement.

1. CAUSE IS DIFFERENT FROM EFFECT.

Gauḍapāda argues that this cannot be the truth, because:

(a) In Indian logic it is customary to offer an example (other than the one being argued), and we have no example of an effect, such as the world, issuing from a cause like the eternal, since nowhere do we see an eternal reality giving birth to something that is temporary. (13a)

(b) If the effect is different from the cause by virtue of not having existed before, we are saying that what lacked existence began to exist, and this is not possible. (31)

(c) Further, if the difference lies in the fact that one is real (at some time) while the other is unreal (at the same time) we must recognize (i) that the unreal cannot be conceived to give birth to another unreality; (ii) that the unreal cannot produce a reality; (iii) that the real cannot give birth to another reality that is different from itself; (iv) that the real cannot produce an unreality. (40)

(d) If the difference is that one is immaterial and the other material (e.g., an immaterial mind and a material body), is it not clear that matter cannot produce the immaterial, nor the immaterial the material? Their difference is such that neither can be responsible for the other. (54)

2. CAUSE IS IDENTICAL WITH EFFECT.

(e) If one partner is mortal and the other immortal (as seems to be the case with Brahman and humans as well as other objects) it is clear that the mortal cannot become immortal and the immortal cannot become mortal, for nothing can change its essential nature. Nothing can exist if it is composed of contradictory characteristics such as mortality-immortality. (7)

(f) As an extension of the last point we may note that Brahman is eternal while effects necessarily have a beginning; they are therefore incompatible—nothing can *really* be both at once. (11)

(g) But if one were to hold that an effect were beginningless (to make it compatible with Brahman) it would still, in the very fact that it arose into particular existence at a given time, represent a transformation of Brahman, and this is absurd because Brahman is changeless and motionless. (12)

(h) If the cause is as transient as the effect (another way of making Brahman and worldly entities compatible so that the reality of both could be affirmed), we must then seek a cause for it, too. And, after that, for the cause of its cause. In other words, we would now be trapped in an infinite regress. (13b)

(i) If the effect did not exist at some time, it never could exist; therefore if one argued that the cause is identical with the effect, one is saying that the cause, as surely as the effect, has never existed! (31)

3. CAUSE IS *BOTH* IDENTICAL AND DIFFERENT FROM EFFECT.

(j) Are they, then, simultaneously and mutually creative? But this does not allow for a beginningless Brahman, and we would again have an infinite regress. (14)

(k) If the effect causes the cause, we have the absurdity of a son generating his own father. (15)

(l) If the effect brings the cause into being, the cause did not formerly exist. A non-existing cause is no cause at all. (17)

(m) To speak of cause and effect implies dependence. If they are identical, it is meaningless to imply such dependence. (18)

4. CAUSE AND EFFECT ARE NOT RELATED.

(n) In this case we would have effects being self-generated, and this is impossible. (23)

These are the arguments Gauḍapāda offers us to prove that *ajātivāda*, non-production, must be correct. Nothing can come into being; there can be no real production, no births. The only conclusion is that all is Brahman, the changeless, and particularity is only apparent, mere *māyā*.

Before moving to the complete text itself, let us record very brief notes concerning these arguments.

(a) This may seem almost an irrelevance to a Western logician, but it has a point. It resembles the objection raised a century or so ago to the argument for the existence of God on the grounds that the world exhibits design and therefore must have a designer, just as a watch must have a watchmaker. The rebuttal is that we can infer a watchmaker from the watch because it is possible to observe watches being made. We could only infer a world-maker from a world if we had similarly observed a world-maker at work somewhere. Without this, we are free to assume that the world, with whatever apparent design it displays, may be merely fortuitous after all.

(b) We have already noted the radical premise that is concealed here. What is not, simply is *not*. It cannot, therefore, begin to be. "Is" and "is not" are contradictions. As one may say, "out of nothing, nothing comes." Of course, this does not eliminate a Being who chooses to exist creatively, within itself, but such a Being is not Gauḍapāda's Brahman, although later it came to be Rāmānuja's.

(c) We may ask, why cannot a real entity produce or give rise to a totally different real entity? The answer that seemed obvious was that two things that have no participation in each other are utterly "other" and neither can be the source of its mate. What is other is always irreparably so;

there is no possible connection. If this is so (and, of course, it is debatable) theories which make God "wholly other" than the world run into difficulties; but this does not apply to pan-en-theism, where what exists cannot be totally other than God, for it exists within His or Her reality.

(d) Modern people who believe that a material organ (the brain) gives birth to immaterial products (ideas) will not find this persuasive.

(e) The Christian idea that the immortal may assume a mortal form is denied here because mortality and immortality are not merely alternative modes that a single entity might take, but are contradictory. If this is rigidly so, we would have to dispense either with Brahman as pervading the world (and the idea of pervading is certainly abandoned by some Vedāntists) or with the world as somehow participating in reality. The latter is a position as unacceptable to later Vedāntists of Rāmānuja's theistic stamp as to Christians, both of whom would reply that to explain the world away is not to explain it, or to account for the impulse to "explain."

(f) This means that they are obviously not simply identical: one cannot impute reality to effects by identifying them with Brahman.

(g) This poses a problem for classical metaphysics in general, Eastern or Western. Process philosophers, on the other hand, counter that the fact of creation shows that God is *not* changeless in all respects, even if He or She is so in character. That is, God is shown by the very fact of world-process to be dynamic even if self-consistent. This would be objectionable to Gauḍapāda because of his assumption that change implies imperfection, a thesis vigorously denied by Process theists.

(h) The infamous "infinite regress" is the terror of philosophy. Thus the West, too, has sought a Primary Cause, an Unmoved Mover, to avoid the slippery path of explanation with no first term. But even an eternity of effects which become causes in their turn is not logically contradictory.

(i) We have already met the notion that what is not can never come to be; this argument merely relates this assumption to causes as well as effects. Perhaps we should note that in all such arguments the assumption is that there is no such thing as growth, transformation; a thing is what it is and remains exactly that. It is a very static ontology that reminds us of those Pacific people who, instead of qualifying a noun like "banana" with adjectives such as "unripe," "ripe," and "over-ripe" create a new word for each of these conditions, evidently on the assumption that at each stage in a banana's life we have a new thing rather than simply a changed thing.

(j) True; but Gauḍapāda has omitted the consideration of asymmetrical simultaneity. One entity might have creativity co-terminous with its being, that is, eternally.

(k) Unthinkable!

(l) True.

(m) Also true.

(n) Theravāda Buddhists seem to have entertained such a notion in their *dhamma* theory; but it is certainly hard to sustain rationally.

In conclusion we may say that if Gauḍapāda's arguments are held to be sound, or sound enough, what they "prove" is either that Brahman, as he conceives of it, alone exists, or that Brahman, as he conceives of it, does not exist. Presumably one must choose one of these outcomes as a matter of faith.

Part Two

THE TEXT: GAUḌAPĀDA'S "QUENCHING THE FIREBRAND" ("ALĀTAŚĀNTI")

INTRODUCTORY NOTE

The following translation follows the Sanskrit text carefully edited by Professor Raghunath Damodar Karmarkar and published in his work, *Gauḍapāda-Kārikā* (Poona: Bhandarkar Oriental Research Institute, 1953). This was officially registered in the Government Oriental Series, class B, as no. 9.

In almost any translation a choice must frequently be made between merely substituting a word in one language for a word in another, and, on the other hand, trying to capture the original *meaning* even at the expense of literal exactitude. The first is much easier to do because the question of meaning (i.e., of determining what the author actually *did* mean) is always open to debate. Nevertheless, in what follows I have chosen to try to be faithful to what seems to have been Gauḍapāda's mind rather than simply putting an English word or words in place of Sanskrit.

It is impossible, therefore, to remove all possibility of scholarly dissent from the rendering offered below. But this version has been fashioned after careful examination of the various previous English translations, and after years of enquiry into the analysis of Gauḍapādan thought by Indian and Western scholars. My *belief* is that Gauḍapāda is dealt with fairly; my *hope* is that the new translation is readable English (as some others were not). One does not have to be an Advaitin to appreciate Gauḍapāda's remarkably vigorous mind and to enjoy crossing swords with him.

The full text of Gauḍapāda's fourth *prakaraṇa* immediately follows. Then, in Part Three, we shall divide this text into sections for the purpose of summary and comment.

ALĀTAŚĀNTI

1. I honor that finest of men who, by means of an understanding as limitless as space and identical with its object, realized the nature of beings, which are like the sky.
2. I honor that which is called the touchless yoga, which leads to the happiness and benefit of all beings and is without contradiction or conflict.
3. Some disputants imagine that births arise from something already existing; others say they spring from non-existence. Thus they argue.
4. No existent can come to birth, and certainly no non-existent can begin to exist. So these disputants, by their mutual contradiction, affirm non origination.
5. We accept without dispute the doctrine of non-origination they proclaim. Know that this is beyond argument.
6. The disputants wish to affirm a birth for that which is unborn. But how can an unborn [and therefore] immortal thing assume mortality?
7. The immortal cannot become mortal nor the mortal immortal, for it is clear that nothing can change its essential nature.
8. If anyone believes that a thing which is inherently immortal becomes mortal, how can they suppose that something constructed to be immortal can remain so?
9. The nature of things is well established as not arbitrarily constructed; innate, natural, not known to surrender its intrinsic character.
10. Everything is, by nature, free from senility and death; yet, fascinated by senility and death, persons move toward them because of preoccupation with them.

11. Those who contend that the cause is identical with the effect are forced [by their argument] to concede that the cause must have had a beginning [since the effect did]. But if the cause begins to exist, it could not be unborn, and something that undergoes birth cannot be eternal.
12. If, on the other hand, you say that cause and effect are identical, [if the cause is eternal] the effect should be beginningless. Otherwise you cannot explain how the cause, which you say is identical with the effect, can be changeless.
13. If anyone were to contend that what is born [the effect] issues from what is unborn [the cause], they could provide no example of such a thing. On the other hand, if the born comes from a source that is also born, you are caught in an infinite regress.
14. If someone argues that the effect is the origin of the cause while the cause, simultaneously, is the origin of the effect, how could the beginninglessness of either be demonstrated?
15. Indeed, those who hold this view of the mutual production of cause and effect seem to say that the son gives birth to the father!
16. If we are to maintain the reality of both cause and effect, we must ascertain the order in which they occur, for if they came into existence at the same time there could be no more causal connection than there is between the two horns of a bull.
17. No cause can be produced from its own effect; and how could a not-yet-existing cause produce an effect?
18. If the cause is held to be accomplished by the effect and the effect by the cause, which comes first? Which of them depends for its origin on the other?
19. Faced with the powerlessness of dualists to reply, their lack of understanding, and their violation of a reasonable concept of sequence, the enlightened person must continue to affirm that there is no origination at all.
20. The observation that seeds cause sprouts needs verification, and whatever lacks verification cannot be offered as "proof" of a theory.
21. The lack of clear understanding about sequence is

the supreme demonstration that there is no real causation. How, indeed, could one fail to see whatever was previous to something that was emerging into existence?

22. Nothing whatever is brought into existence, whether from itself or from something else: nothing at all! Not anything existent, non-existent or both is ever originated.
23. Further, a cause is not born from something that is itself beginningless, nor can an effect arise simply by its own power. Whatever has no beginning is obviously also without a cause.
24. Our naming of things depends on an objective stimulus [observer and observed must both exist or neither does]. For this reason, and because of the experience of bondage to ignorance, some base their philosophy on an acceptance of real objects.
25. Empirical observation supports the idea that knowledge is stimulated by an objective cause, but a true perception of things sustains the view that there is no genuine cause.
26. The mind does not actually make contact with real objects or even objective images. Objects do not exist, and therefore images are not outside the mind itself.
27. Not in the past, present, or future does the mind really contact anything to "cause" its contents. Lacking such a cause, then, how can mistaken impressions be born?
28. Thus, neither the mind nor its content is born; whoever seeks a beginning may as well search for the footprints of birds in the sky.
29. Some say that the unborn is born. Non-birth, however, is its very nature, and there is no way a thing can alter its nature.
30. If the cycle of birth and death [*samsāra*] were beginningless, it could have no end [for the beginningless is eternal], and if deliverance from it had a beginning, it would necessarily also have an end [since it would be finite].
31. Anything that lacked existence at some time in the past and will fail to exist at some time in the future

must also be non-existent in the present. The things we commonly treat as real are no more than illusions.

32. The belief that objects we see are uniquely practical things is contradicted by our experience of practical things in our dreams. Thus tradition holds them to be merely unreal because they begin and end.
33. Dream-objects are illusions, existing only within our bodies. How could a perception of real objects be obtained within that narrow sphere?
34. It is not possible that the dreamer actually went to where the dream-objects seemed to be, because the time spent dreaming is too short. And when the dreamer awakens, he finds he is not really where he dreamed he was.
35. One dreams of talking to friends, but on awakening finds that one has not done so. We acquire things in dreams, but cannot find them when we awaken.
36. Our bodies, as they appear in dreams, are shown to be unreal by the fact that our actual bodies can be seen to be different. Similarly, all the mind's images are unreal.
37. Because things seen in dreams resemble things seen when we are awake, wakeful experience is thought to be the basis of dream experience. Thus wakeful experience, supposed to be the inspiration of dreams, is believed by the dreamer to be real—even though it is his own experience alone.
38. Because origination cannot be proven, all things are declared to be unborn. Certainly the real cannot give birth to the unreal.
39. If we are sufficiently impressed by an unreal object "seen" when we are awake, we may then dream about it. But seeing it in a dream does not ensure that we will find it again when we awaken.
40. An unreal cannot cause another unreal to exist, and the real cannot spring from the unreal. But the real also cannot cause the arising of a different real. How could the real, then, give birth to the unreal?
41. Just as, even when awake, one may seem to encounter impossible objects because of misperception, in dream one sees objects only because of false perception.

42. The enlightened one teaches things about "origination" for the sake of realists who are persuaded by their ordinary experience, by conventional opinion, or by their fear of the idea that there is no origination of anything.
43. Those who go astray because of their perceptions and their fear of non-origination are not deeply wounded by evil consequences of their error; such consequences are minor.
44. Just as one may speak of an illusory elephant as if it were real simply because it seems to be seen and it seems to behave as one would expect, so because they seem to be seen and conform to expectation one speaks of things existing.
45. What appear to be origination, movement, and things are really the unborn itself, the unmoving, substanceless consciousness, peaceful and non-dual.
46. The mind is never born, and therefore its objects are said in scripture to be also without origination. Those who grasp this clearly do not fall into error.
47. Just as the waving of a firebrand seems to produce straight or crooked lines, so the movement of consciousness seems to produce perceiver and perceived.
48. When a firebrand is not waved it presents no apparent patterns and is originating nothing. Similarly, unwavering consciousness presents no appearances and is free from originating anything.
49. When a firebrand is waving, the images do not come to it from somewhere else. When it ceases to wave they do not go elsewhere. Nor do they retreat into the firebrand.
50. They do not actually emerge from the firebrand, for they have no substance. This is true of consciousness' images too: mere appearance is always only that.
51. When consciousness is agitated, the images do not come to it from somewhere else. When the agitation ceases, they do not go elsewhere or retreat into consciousness.
52. They do not emerge from consciousness, for they have no substance. They are always incomprehensible because no cause-effect connection exists.

53. Substance [if it exists] may cause substance, and something insubstantial may be the cause of something else of the same kind, but neither substance nor the insubstantial are suitable categories for entities.
54. The mind is not produced from material things and does not itself produce such things. The wise, therefore, are driven to a doctrine of the non-occurrence of causation.
55. So long as a person believes in cause and effect, these will seem to occur; but when one abandons belief in causes and effects, they vanish entirely.
56. So long as one is possessed by notions of cause and effect, the cycle of birth, death, and rebirth persists. When one no longer believes in causation, the cycle is ended.
57. Everything in ordinary experience has a beginning and is therefore not eternal. By contrast, whatever really exists is without beginning and therefore is also endless.
58. Things are said to begin, but their beginning is not real: rather, it is like an illusion—but an illusion that itself does not really exist.
59. A sprout that grows from an illusory seed must itself be an illusion, and it therefore cannot properly be said to be either permanent or even temporary. The same is true of other things.
60. One simply cannot apply the terms "eternal" or "non-eternal"to objects that never really begin to exist. When words fail, one cannot employ distinctions.
61 Just as the mind, when we are dreaming, moves in the illusion of duality, so even in the waking state duality is an illusion presented by the mind.
62. In dreams the non-dual mind undoubtedly appears to be divided. Similarly, in wakefulness too the non-dual seems to be divided.
63. The creatures we seem to see in dreams, whether womb-born or born of moisture, moving everywhere...
64. are to be seen only in the dreamer's mind and do not exist apart from it. So, too, even the dreamer's mind itself is only imagined to have an independent existence.

65. It is the same with womb- or moisture-born creatures seen in our waking state, moving everywhere...
66. they can be seen only by the mind of the wakeful person, and apart from it they have no existence. And the wakeful mind itself is only imagined to have independent reality.
67. Both perceiver and perceived are established by the perceiving act alone. What, then, is independently real? Nothing! Individual minds are devoid of marks of reality and are imagined by their own thoughts.
68. As dream-produced individuals [*jīvas*] are born and die, so all individuals are and yet are not.
69. As a conjuror's individual is born and dies, so all individuals are and yet are not.
70. As a person created by [yogic] magic is born and dies, so all persons are and yet are not.
71. No individual entity is born: no such beginning ever really takes place. This is the highest truth: nothing whatever is originated.
72. The duality of subject and object is only an agitation of the mind itself. The mind is unrelated to any object. Thus it is said to be always unattached.
73. Whatever depends on empirical experience does not really exist. It seems to exist only within that empirical experience on which it is dependent.
74. So everything that ordinary experience judges to be unoriginated is not really so; dependent things arise in ordinary experience.
75. Where there is conviction about the unreality of things there is no experience of duality. Whoever understands the unreality of duality is free from it, for its cause has been destroyed.
76. A mind that is not associated with causes, whether these are superior, inferior, or middling, is not born. In the absense of a cause, how could there be an effect?
77. Since the mind is free from birth or any causal relation,everything else is also unoriginated; there is no duality.
78. If we understand true causelessness, and find no cause, we achieve a state without sorrow, desire, or fear.

79. If the mind is attached to unreal objects, it pursues such things. When it realizes that these objects are unreal,it turns back from them and escapes attachment.
80. A mind thus turned back and inactive is, indeed, without movement. This is the condition of the enlightened ones: unconditioned, unborn, and non-dual.
81. Unborn, sleepless, dreamless, this enlightened mind is self-illuminating. By its very nature it is forever luminous.
82. But if a mind turns toward individual objects, it loses bliss and discovers suffering. The Lord is not, then, easily recovered.
83. [This is because] the misguided person conceals reality with speculation whether it is, is not, is and is not, or neither is nor is not. Or he wonders whether reality moves or is still, is both moving and still, or is neither.
84. These are the four logical alternatives by which people try to understand. That person is all-knowing who recognizes that the luminous one is not to be grasped by such speculation.
85. If one attains omniscient non-dual wisdom in its fullness,appropriate for a Brahmin, without beginning, middle, or end, what more could one want?
86. This Brahmin discipline is said to be a natural means of introverted tranquility, since nature itself is under control. He who understands this may attain peace.
87. A waking state may be acknowledged in which duality entailing actual objects is envisioned. There is also a dreaming state where none of the imagined objects are tangible.
88. And there is a further state, traditionally called dreamless sleep, wherein neither object nor images can be found.The enlightened ones affirm knowledge, the object known,and that which should be known.
89. When the trio of knowledge and its kinds of content are understood in the correct order, omniscience spontaneously awakens in a person of great intellect.
90. From the Agrayāṇa we learn what ought to be avoided, whatought to be realized, what ought to be

appropriated, and what ought to be rendered ineffective. Except that which ought to be realized, these are all traditionally recognized as figments of mundane perception.

91. Everything should be known to be, by nature, without a beginning, like space. No multiplicity exists anywhere.
92. All things are, by their true nature, established as *Ādibuddha*. Whoever rests content with this is able to achieve immortality.
93. All entities are intrinsically peaceful, unoriginated and perfectly free from anxiety. They are always the same and are not different from each other. They are unborn, identical and perfect.
94. But there is never peace for those who believe in otherness; those who affirm a doctrine of individuality sink into separateness and are traditionally described as pitiful.
95. Those, on the other hand, who wish to be established in the unborn sameness, whoever they are, are indeed persons of great understanding in the world. The world in general does not penetrate such understanding.
96. The unoriginating knowledge is thought of as not making contact with objects which are themselves unoriginated. As it lacks such contact, it is said to be unconditioned.
97. If a difference of even the slightest degree is affirmed by the unwise, there is no consistent detachment and therefore no penetrating of the veil of illusion.
98. All beings are by nature free of accretions and are unstained. The Masters say they are free and pure light from the first.
99. According to the enlightened one, understanding never touches objects, and nothing touches understanding. The Buddha has not said this.
100. Having attained the supreme state which is profound, birthless, void of distinctions, imperishable and always the same, we offer it all possible honor.

Part Three

COMMENTARY

COMMENTARY

For the purpose of comment, we shall divide the text into twenty-one sections of varying lengths. The verses of each section will be set out first, and then a selective commentary will follow.

At the head of each set of verses will be a succinct summary of their main content enclosed in brackets.

I. VERSES 1–2

{The enlightened master and his yoga are to be honored.}

1. I honor that finest of men who, by means of an understanding as limitless as space and identical with its object, realized the nature of beings, which are like the sky.
2. I honor that which is called the touchless yoga, which leads to the happiness and benefit of all beings and is without contradiction or conflict.

These introductory verses have been offered by some as evidence that we have, in this *prakaraṇa* an entirely independent work. If we simply began a fourth chapter of a continuing exposition, it is argued, we would hardly expect a new salutation of this sort. This is not conclusive, but it carries weight because none of the other *prakaraṇas* begin in the same fashion. Indeed, the surprising fact that even the first lacks such an introduction has led some to suggest that this *prakaraṇa* alone is the work of Gauḍapāda, but this is a position that seems improbable because near contemporaries evidently believed Gauḍapāda had also written the rest.

A more earnestly contested issue is the identity of that "best of bipeds" (which we render "finest of men"). It is, presumably, someone from whom Gauḍapāda learned much of what he had to teach. Thus Ānandagiri refers it to Guaḍapāda's own personal *guru*, Nārāyana, but it is a little surprising, if this is correct, that the verse does not mention this man's name. Furthermore, he uses a form of expression most commonly employed to honor Gautama, the Buddha. In view of this, and the obvious use of Buddhist terms and ideas throughout the work, many have believed that it is the Buddha who is intended here. This issue, too, must remain in doubt.

The "touchless yoga" of verse 2 (*asparśa yoga*) means, according to Śaṅkara's comment on the verse, a yoga that eliminates all sense of contact with objects by intense concentration on Brahman. It is therefore a yoga that eliminates all relativity. With regard to verse 1, Śaṅkara remarks that the knowledge that is as limitless as space is a knowledge that pervades everywhere, as space does. In other words, it is a knowledge that is ubiquitous and therefore leaves room for nothing else—it *is* its object. This, in turn, is why this yoga and its knowledge are "beyond dispute." Such knowledge is not broken up by objective content (it is not a knowledge *about* things but a kind of knowledge that actually dissolves distinctions and absorbs all). It could never, therefore enter into or be the object of dispute. Obviously, it is not a philosophical position, but a state of mind.

Despite Śaṅkara, all this might as readily be said of certain kinds of Buddhist yoga as well as that centered on Brahman.

II. VERSES 3–9

{Nothing can change its nature, and therefore nothing can come into being either from an existent or from non-existence.}

3. Some disputants imagine that births arise from something already existing; others say they spring from non-existence. Thus they argue.

4. No existent can come to birth, and certainly no nonexistent can begin to exist. So these disputants, by their mutual contradiction, affirm non-origination.
5. We accept without dispute the doctrine of non-origination they proclaim. Know that this is beyond argument.
6. The disputants wish to affirm a birth for that which is unborn. But how can an unborn [and therefore] immortal thing assume mortality?
7. The immortal cannot become mortal nor the mortal immortal, for it is clear that nothing can change its essential nature.
8. If anyone believes that a thing which is inherently immortal becomes mortal, how can they suppose that something constructed to be immortal can remain so?
9. The nature of things is well established as not arbitrarily constructed; innate, natural, not known to surrender its intrinsic character.

The disputants referred to here are the Sāṃkhyans, on the one hand, and Vaiśeṣikas, Nayāyikas and perhaps others who, accepting the reality of causation, had to discuss whether the effect had previously existed within the cause or was an entirely new thing. Gauḍapāda argues that their fruitless debate indicates that neither position can be sustained. If something already is, it cannot begin to be (so cannot really be an effect in the strict sense), but if something does not exist, it cannot begin to do so.

Clearly Gauḍapāda rests on an assumption that no such notion as the movement from potency to actuality can occur and, therefore, nothing can change its nature, even if its appearance might seem to change. Verses 6–8 repeat what was already said in *prakaraṇa* III.20–22, and simply prepare for the statement in verse 9: nothing ever changes its nature.

If nothing changes, there is no novelty, no innovation or, in his preferred word, no birth or production of anything. Grant this premise, and Gauḍapāda's further arguments in this *prakaraṇa* gain enormous weight. Obviously not everyone, then or now, will grant him his premise! The transition of energy to matter and *vice versa*, or even Aristotle's defense of potency present alternative perspectives.

III. VERSE 10

{We are actually free from senility and death, yet seem to suffer them because of infatuation.}

10. Everything is, by nature, free from senility and death; yet, fascinated by senility and death, persons move toward them because of preoccupation with them.

"Everything" refers particularly to all *jīvas*, all persons in their false, limited self-understanding. Being really the one eternal *Ātman*, they are actually beyond change and decay, but they do not realize this. Thus they fear life's diminishments and their very fear causes them to seem to suffer the ravages from which they recoil. Our fear and our acceptance of death and aging as if they were inescapable facts is actually ridiculous, since such events do not even exist for our inner and real being.

IV. VERSES 11–23

{That no real birth or production occurs is proved by the failure of all causal theories. It can be shown that cause is not identical with effect, yet effects do not really come from causes and causes and effects cannot be mutually productive.}

11. Those who contend that the cause is identical with the effect are forced [by their argument] to concede that the cause must have had a beginning [since the effect did]. But if the cause begins to exist, it could not be unborn, and something that undergoes birth cannot be eternal.
12. If, on the other hand, you say that cause and

effect are identical, [if the cause is eternal] the effect should be beginningless. Otherwise you cannot explain how the cause, which you say is identical with the effect, can be changeless.

13. If anyone were to contend that what is born [the-effect] issues from what is unborn [the cause], they could provide no example of such a thing. On the other hand, if the born comes from a source that is also born, you are caught in an infinite regress.
14. If someone argues that the effect is the origin of the cause while the cause, simultaneously, is the origin of the effect, how could the beginninglessness of either be demonstrated?
15. Indeed, those who hold this view of the mutual production of cause and effect seem to say that the son gives birth to the father!
16. If we are to maintain the reality of both cause and effect, we must ascertain the order in which they occur, for if they came into existence at the same time there could be no more causal connection than there is between the two horns of a bull.
17. No cause can be produced from its own effect; and how could a not-yet-existing cause produce an effect?
18. If the cause is held to be accomplished by the effect and the effect by the cause, which comes first? Which of them depends for its origin on the other?
19. Faced with the powerlessness of dualists to reply, their lack of understanding, and their violation of a reasonable concept of sequence, the enlightened person must continue to affirm that there is no origination at all.
20. The observation that seeds cause sprouts needs verification, and whatever lacks verification cannot be offered as "proof" of a theory.
21. The lack of clear understanding about sequence is the supreme demonstration that there is no real causation. How, indeed, could one fail to see whatever was previous to something that was emerging into existence?

22. Nothing whatever is brought into existence, whether from itself or from something else: nothing at all! Not anything existent, non-existent or both is ever originated.
23. Further, a cause is not born from something that is itself beginningless, nor can an effect simply arise by its own power. Whatever has no beginning is obviously also without a cause.

This section is central to Gauḍapāda's thesis. If causality is real—that is, if there is a genuine production of things—there are only several possible relations of cause and effect, of producer and product, and Gauḍapāda tries to show that all these options are finally contradictory.

The possibilities are:

(a) Cause produces effect.
(b) Effect produces cause.
(c) They produce each other.
(d) They arise at the same time.

Some scholars, including Vidhushekhara Bhattacharya, have noted that the first of these possibilities seems to lack treatment by Gauḍapāda and have wondered whether this means that one or more verses have been accidentally lost as the text was copied, but Karmarkar finds this contention groundless. He believes that the first part of verse 19 should be treated as meaning that dualists see cause and effect as different, in which case neither can account for the other.[32] Karmarkar's position is strengthened by verse 20 where it is denied that the observation that sprouts seem to emerge from seeds is "proof" of production. One might wonder whether Gauḍapāda's point is that the seed-sprout example will not satisfy the Sāṁkhyan who wants an *eternal* cause (for the seed was itself not eternal but arose from a previous plant and so on *ad infinitum*) or, as David Hume might have said, that the regularity with which sprouts follow seeds is not proof of a necessary causal relation: there might be another explanation. I think he is refuting the Sāṁkhyans, and I do not find Karmarkar's interpretation of verse 19 persuasive. But at least it may be said that, in various places, he rejects the notion of an infinite regress, and this means that he finds the idea of a beginningless and endless series of dependent products incoherent.

The second of our options (effects produce causes) is lampooned. This means that the son generates the father (verse 15). The third is dealt with by saying that if cause and effect produce each other, one could not show that either is original or immortal, and we are back with an infinite regress. The fourth option is dismissed. Simultaneous things would have to be shown to have a causal relationship: the two horns of a cow arise simultaneously, but are surely not in causal relation. Buddhists had already argued that cause and effect cannot be ascribed to things that arise at the same time. Candrakirti, for example, had maintained that when simultaneous things arise (such as left and right hands or feet) one cannot affirm a causal relation.[33]

The force of this section depends on the assumption that an endless (or beginningless) series of dependent events is not self-explanatory. If birth or production is to become explicable something must *give* birth or produce, and if we are to avoid the infinite regress, something must support the series without itself being born or dependent.

In verses 11 and 12 he again takes the Sāṁkhyans to task. They accept the idea of an immutable cause, yet argue that it somehow becomes the effect; but if it does so, it cannot be immutable. The Sāṁkhyans seem to want too much: the "cause-effect" must be changeless yet emergent! Śaṅkara, commenting on this verse, uses a charming metaphor to clarify the point: you cannot divide the cause into an immortal and a mortal part any more than you can split a hen, cooking one part but keeping the other to lay eggs!

In Indian logic it was generally recognized that only three possibilities exist for the order of a causal sequence. The cause precedes the effect (*pūrva-krama* or "priority"), the effect precedes the cause (*apara-krama* or "posteriority"), and thirdly, they arise together (*saha-krama* or "simultaneity"). In verse 21 Gauḍapāda claims that none of these makes sense, and therefore the entire notion of cause and effect is worthless.

Verse 22 echoes a comment by Nāgārjuna who asks, in *Mūlamādhyamakārikā* I.7, "How can the beginning of things be asserted if nothing can be found that can be said to exist, to fail to exist, or both?" Śaṅkara's comment is that if something were immortal it would surely not indulge in superfluous productivity. Presumably he bases his remark on the idea that the immortal must also be perfect, and the perfect needs nothing more than itself. On the other hand, he says, anything that does not exist cannot begin to do so because this event would change its fundamental nature (that is, its non-existence). Finally, it is clear that nothing can be both existent and non-existent because these terms are contradictory.

Verse 23 is offered as a clinching argument. Nothing arises through its own power to come into existence, yet nothing can be said really to be born (really to be produced) from what is beginningless. Suppose we hold that the sequence of events that make up the history of the universe is without a beginning; then it is also without a cause. How, then, could it come to be? Surely not through its own power, for nothing *begins* to exist without a producer. Yet, in the case of the universe, no adequate producer can be found within it. It would need a producer outside itself, and one that was not itself caused, one that had no beginning. But such a producer, being without a beginning itself, would have to be changeless because whatever changes is vulnerable to corruption and cannot be thought to be either self-sufficient or immortal—that is, beginningless. But a changeless producer is a contradiction, since the very act of production effects a change in the producer.

In short, mortal producers or causes cannot account for the universe, but the immortal cannot be thought to produce real objects. This is not nihilism; there *is* a reality.

But Gauḍapāda's point is that whatever is finally real cannot be a real producer of real things and therefore notions of production, or causality, are fallacious.

Either there is a "reality" but it does not produce any other real things, and the universe must be understood in some other way (i.e., it is *ajāti*, unborn); or there is nothing at all, which is absurd. The universe must, then, in some way be not other than the real itself, but this means it is "really" changeless and single (for the assumption is that a plurality of things is always in tension and not eternal). The appearance of the world as a sequence of produced entities and events must be an illusion.

We should recognize, however, that some philosophers have found an eternal series without a primary uncaused cause to be no less imaginable than Gauḍapāda's uncaused "reality" which is the basis, somehow, of an illusory world. And theologians, such as St. Thomas, have not considered the notion of an intrinsically creative God necessarily to imply that God's imperfection.

V. VERSES 24–25

{Commmon experience, however, leads empiricism falsely to believe that objects are real.}

24. Our naming of things depends on an objective stimulus [observer and observed must both exist or neither does]. For this reason, and because of the experience of bondage to ignorance, some base their philosophy on an acceptance of real objects.
25. Empirical observation supports the idea that knowledge is stimulated by an objective cause, but a true perception of things sustains the view that there is no genuine cause.

Evidently anticipating an objection to what has been said, Gauḍapāda himself raises a question—probably one he had dealt with often enough in debate. Commonsense realism maintains that subjective states are caused by objective facts. We sense many things and we experience pain: it is unreasonable to suppose that an intrinsically pure and untroubled consciousness, such as Brahman, would invent or project such things to disturb it. As Śaṅkara remarks, in his gloss on this verse, subjective variations are inexplicable unless they are provoked by objective variety.

But verse 25 is Gauḍapāda's response. He will show that objectivity is itself an impossible concept to maintain, and therefore objects will be seen not to be a cause of subjective impressions.

VI. VERSES 26–29

{The mind is unborn and changeless in essence, and makes no actual contact with anything outside it.}

26. The mind does not actually make contact with real objects or even objective images. Objects do not exist, and therefore images are not outside the mind itself.
27. Not in the past, present, or future does the mind really contact anything to "cause" its contents. Lacking such a cause, then, how can mistaken impressions be born?
28. Thus, neither the mind nor its content is born; whoever seeks a beginning may as well search for the footprints of birds in the sky.
29. Some say that the unborn is born. Non-birth, however, is its very nature, and there is no way a thing can alter its nature.

The force of the argument here depends on the premise that whatever once was not cannot now begin to be. Some had argued that the mind, which is identified with its content, comes into being through the stimulus of an object, but it is obvious that no actual object enters into the mind; we gain only mental impressions. Further, if objects do not really exist, as Gauḍapāda holds, our impressions cannot arise from such a source but must belong entirely to the mind's own effort.

Some had said that the difference between accurate and inaccurate impressions lay in the fact that the mind sometimes falsely imposed the impression gained from a previously encountered object onto a new object. But if there are no real objects, in past, present, or future, this cannot be the case. False and "true" impressions are alike in being without objective cause.

Verse 28 brings us to a logical inference from this. If there are no "real" objects to cause the mind (that is, its ideas) to be born we can take a further step. The thinking mind itself, the perceiving intellect, is no more a true product, a real, substantial entity, than the objects it seems to contain. In other words, both the alleged objects and the mind that is supposed to perceive them are no more than ideas. The rational mind can no more explain itself into reality than it can justify its belief in objects. Śaṅkara uses the "footprints in the sky" metaphor in his *bhāṣya* on the *Bṛhadāraṇyaka* V.4–6, but an earlier use of it may be found in the Buddhist *Dhammapada* 93.

Verse 29 gives us the conclusion. There is an "unborn" for Gauḍapāda: it is Brahman. But the "real" mind, the reality behind the false, perceiving mind, whose arising cannot be explained, must also be unborn, and this means that it can be nothing but Brahman. Moreover, since nothing can change its nature, neither Brahman nor the true mind (*Ātman*) can be identified simply with perception or reason, and therefore the mind that seems to arise in its perception of objects must be as illusory as the objects of the world themselves.

An objection suggests itself at once, and we shall note it, but as Gauḍapāda does not deal with it here we shall wait to see whether he satisfies us later.

Even if objective knowledge and rational thought are less than real—even if objects and ideas are illusions—the illusions must exist somewhere. Gauḍapāda evidently has the idea that he is writing something. Who, then, is the real bearer of the illusion? Not my own individual mind, for it *is* illusion. Can it be that Brahman is deceived by illusion? Could it be tricked by its own imagination?

We may also note that we find here a typical Vedāntic identification of Brahman and *Ātman*. An objector might wonder why these could not be separate realities, but for Gauḍapāda there can be only one unborn reality because if there were two they would be mutually limiting, and limited things are vulnerable. Our final security lies in this identification.

VII. VERSES 30–31

{*Samsāra*, however, cannot be beginningless or it would have no end; and deliverance from it cannot begin, or it would cease. *Samsāric* things are illusions.}

30. If the cycle of birth and death (*samsāra*) were beginningless, it could have no end [for beginninglessness is eternal], and if deliverance from it had a beginning it would necessarily also have an end [since it would be finite].
31. Anything that lacked existence at some time in the past and will fail to exist at some time in the future must also be non-existent in the present. The things we commonly treat as real are no more than illusions.

We have just been told that Brahman (and therefore *Ātman*) is beginningless and endless. The question arises next, what is the status of *samsāra*, the ordinarily perceived and experienced world?

There were those who said that it was also beginningless but would eventually cease to function or appear. Many Mahāyāna Buddhists appeared to hold such a view. On the other hand, some said that *mokṣa* (deliverance, release, liberation, salvation) must have a beginning, but would thereafter never end.

Both these propositions are offensive to Gauḍapāda's logical assumption that whatever exists at any time exists always and whatever fails to exist at any time can never really do so because nothing can change its nature and existence cannot become non-existence or *vice versa*.

An objector might say that this ignores experience. Any of us might know a moment when the light dawns and we "see" the truth; surely that means that liberation has begun. If, as is possible in theory at least, every sentient being was at last thus liberated, surely *samsāra* would end. Both *mokṣa* and *samsāra*, then, are alike in being less than eternal and, that being so, it is reasonable to suppose that both have a beginning and both may end.

In his comment on the verse Ānandagiri uses a metaphor.[34] If the sun were sentient, it would say that there is never an alternation of night and day: there is neither dawn nor evening, for all is constantly bright with noonday radiance. It is we, who are not experiencing ourselves as the sun, who see transitions from darkness to light. Similarly, for Brahman there is no alternation between *samsāra* and *mokṣa*. The experience of awakening, and the error from which this delivers us, are as false for Brahman as dawn and sunset are for the sun. This is the sense in which, as many Buddhists said, "*samsāra* is *nirvāṇa*." *We* experience these as different, but from the perspective of truth itself, there is no movement, no change.

VIII. 32–41

{As dream-objects are unreal, so are those of wakeful experience.}

32. The belief that objects we see are uniquely practical things is contradicted by our experience of practical things in our dreams. Thus tradition holds them to be merely unreal because they begin and end.
33. Dream-objects are illusions, existing only within our bodies. How could a perception of real objects be obtained within that narrow sphere?
34. It is not possible that the dreamer actually went to where the dream-objects seemed to be, because the time spent dreaming is too short. And when the dreamer awakens, he finds he is not really where he dreamed he was.

35. One dreams of talking to friends, but on awakening finds that one has not done so. We acquire things in dreams, but cannot find them when we awaken.
36. Our bodies, as they appear in dreams, are shown to be unreal by the fact that our actual bodies can be seen to be different. Similarly, all the mind's images are unreal.
37. Because things seen in dreams resemble things seen when we are awake, wakeful experience is thought to be the basis of dream experience. Thus wakeful experience, supposed to be the inspiration of dreams, is believed by the dreamer to be real—even though it is his own experience alone.
38. Because origination cannot be proven, all things are declared to be unborn. Certainly the real cannot give birth to the unreal.
39. If we are sufficiently impressed by an unreal object "seen" when we are awake, we may then dream about it. But seeing it in a dream does not ensure that we will find it again when we awaken.
40. An unreal cannot cause another unreal to exist, and the real cannot spring from the unreal. But the real also cannot cause the arising of a different real. How could the real, then, give birth to the unreal?
41. Just as, even when awake, one may seem to encounter impossible objects because of misperception, in dream one sees objects only because of false perception.

It is a common assumption that objects seen when we are alert have a reality that dream images lack. Gauḍapāda is anxious to refute this. Anything that is truly "real," in Gauḍapāda's opinion, is necessarily unchanging—always the same. It will always be wherever it is and as it is. But when we sleep, the objects of our waking life vanish.

An objector may say that nevertheless what establishes the reality of our "waking" objects is the fact that they have practical value: we can make use of them. Ah, replies Gauḍapāda, but even this usefulness vanishes when we sleep. As Karmarkar puts it, "a dreamer sleeping in a house dreams that he is out in the open, getting all wet in the rain; the *saprayojanatā* (usefulness, practical reality) of the house is thus set at naught in the dream."[35] Thus dreaming contradicts all waking impressions. They are as discredited by their absense in our dreams as our dream images are when we awaken.

In several verses, Gauḍapāda now argues that it is foolish to accept dreams as representing realities because such creations of the imagination are easily shown to be incompatible with common sense: e.g., the dream of a castle occurs entirely within us, but obviously the small space of our bodies cannot contain a real castle.

In verse 37 Gauḍapāda presses his point by what seems to be a borrowing of an argument used by Mādhyamikan Buddhists against their Sautrāntika rivals. The latter had said that the reality of an object was confirmed by a clear, veridical observation, but the Mādhyamikans replied that we can imagine we see non-existent things (perhaps because of optical illusion) so that wakeful perception is no more confirmatory than dreams.[36]

Śaṅkara, in his gloss on verse 39, pushes the argument a step further. Not only is it true that we may dream about something that impressed us while we were awake but we may even dream about something that appeared to our wakeful eyes only by error, such as a snake which we "saw" instead of a rope. Moreover, we often fail to dream of things that impressed us when we were awake. It must be clear, then, that the argument that dreams depend on actual things that really exist and were perceived in our wakefulness falls to the ground.

Verse 40 reiterates Gauḍapāda's argument for the non-reality of causation, and verse 41 brings us to the conclusion that since origination cannot be demonstrated, and empirical evidence is no more reliable than dreams, *all* entities and events must be understood to be illusions.

The main argument of this section (which occurs previously in *prakaraṇa* 2) can be restated in the form of traditional Hindu logic. It would then appear in this mode:

> *Pratijñā* (conclusion to be reached): Objects seen when we are awake are unreal.
>
> *Hetu* (reason for this): Because they are known by perception.
>
> *Dṛṣṭānta* (example): As are the objects we seem to see in dreams.
>
> *Hetūpanaya* (argument): Just as dream objects are known to be false, so are those of wakeful experience since they, also, are perceived by the mind in the same subjective way.
>
> *Nigamana* (conclusion): Therefore wakeful perceptions of objects are false or, objects seen when we are awake are unreal.

Gauḍapāda's arguments may not convince everyone, but his conclusion is clear: things seen in dreams or waking states are equally false; they are *māyā*—illusion.

The objector may now be growing impatient for an answer to the question, who, then, is creating the illusions? As we have said, it cannot be the individual person, for she or he, as individual, is within the illusion. Gauḍapāda does not deal with this directly here, perhaps because he has answered the question elsewhere. In *prakaraṇa* 2:12 he made the bold assertion that "the self-luminous *Ātman* itself, by means of its own *māyā*, imagines within itself all objects and experiences." This, however, is a solution to the problem that Śaṅkara eventually rejected, for it makes Brahman the efficient cause of the illusion, and this implies either that Brahman actively creates it or is victimized by it—neither of which is acceptable if Brahman is to be considered perfect, undeceived, unchanging, and inactive because in need of nothing.

Śaṅkara's own solution, however, cannot be said to be any more successful. He argued that all perceived objects were falsely superimposed or projected onto Brahman. But again we must ask whether Brahman does the superimposing, whether this process is an independent fact that exists "outside" Brahman, or whether we ourselves do it.

The last possibility will not hold unless a superimposition can superimpose! And even then, who can it be that produces the first superimposition of the subsequent superimposer? The second falls beneath the criticism that Brahman is infinite and can be limited by no independent fact. And Brahman cannot itself create the superimposition, for then it would be active and to be active is to change.

IX. VERSES 42–43

{It is true that enlightened Masters may talk about "origination" but this is only a useful device in their hands, and it does no real harm to those who take it seriously.}

42. The enlightened one teaches things about "origination" for the sake of realists who are persuaded by their ordinary experience, by conventional opinion, or by their fear of the idea that there is no origination of anything.
43. Those who go astray because of their perceptions and their fear of non-origination are not deeply wounded by evil consequences of their error; such consequences are minor.

There can be no doubt that many authoritative writings in India speak as if causality really occurs and genuine, substantial things thereby come to birth. This, after all, is the basis of the many religious rites taught in the Vedas. Further, the Buddha had said things about origination, even (according to tradition) presenting a theory of twelve links in a chain of mutually dependent and mutually productive elements of experience. How, then, can Gauḍapāda teach *ajātivāda*, the doctrine of no production?

The answer is simple. The enlightened ("*buddha*": it is debated whether this means Gautama Buddha or just enlightened masters in general) may use such terms and ideas, but only for the benefit of people too timid to enter into the full truth. Whatever is taught about origination by the wise is helpful for those who do not dare challenge their notions of self and world in the radical way proposed by non-dualism. As Śaṅkara puts it, the *śrotriyas* who hold to the reality of forms are dull folk who fear to admit that there is no real causation because they think this implies their own annihilation. It is a kindness to allow them to allay their fears. But we should be of good cheer; such simple people may be weak but are not evil, and their present error about origination will not bear decisively terrible consequences, such as eternal exclusion from truth. Professor Karmarkar betrays his prejudices in commenting on this verse, as he says, "They are not *nāstikas* (heretics) like the Cārvākas or Buddhists, and with luck, they can ultimately see their way to believing in the *ajātivāda*."[37] Ānandagiri, discussing Bhagavad Gītā X.7, remarks that the knowledge of *saguna* Brahman (Brahman with divine attributes superimposed) may be erroneous but helpful because it is the gateway to a mature awareness of *nirguna* (unconditioned, qualityless) Brahman. This seems to be the point of this verse.

X. VERSES 44–52

{Existents only seem to be real, as do the shapes created by a whirling firebrand.}

44. Just as one may speak of an illusory elephant as if it were real simply because it seems to be seen and it seems to behave as one would expect, so because they seem to be seen and conform to expectation one speaks of things existing.
45. What appear to be origination, movement, and things are really the unborn itself, the unmoving, substanceless consciousness, peaceful and non-dual.
46. The mind is never born, and therefore its objects are said in scripture to be also without origination. Those who grasp this clearly do not fall into error.
47. Just as the waving of a firebrand seems to produce straight or crooked lines, so the movement of consciousness seems to produce perceiver and perceived.

48. When a firebrand is not waved it presents no apparent patterns and is originating nothing. Similarly, unwavering consciousness presents no appearances and is free from originating anything.
49. When a firebrand is waving, the images do not come to it from somewhere else. When it ceases to wave they do not go elsewhere. Nor do they retreat into the firebrand.
50. They do not actually emerge from the firebrand, for they have no substance. This is true of consciousness' images too: mere appearance is always only that.
51. When consciousness is agitated, the images do not come to it from somewhere else. When the agitation ceases, they do not go elsewhere or retreat into consciousness.
52. They do not emerge from consciousness, for they have no substance. They are always incomprehensible because no cause-effect connection exists.

We can imagine the troubled objector: Things seen when we are fully awake *must* have reality because so many of them are practical things that we can put to use. Gauḍapāda replies that a skilful conjuror in the village market place might produce equally "useful" things—an elephant, for example! The entranced audience may watch this beast perform many tasks or tricks. Then, with a smile and a wave of his hand, the conjuror dismisses it to oblivion and we laugh because we have been deceived. If we were intelligent, we knew all along that there was trickery here, and that only the conjuror himself truly stood before us. Similarly, as verse 45 says, behind the illusion of a moving world the only real thing is unmoving consciousness itself.

But if Brahman, the true reality, is motionless and undivided, its apparent "products" can have no real origin (since it does not move or change); and what is limitless and undivided leaves no room for other entities.

Verse 47 brings us the metaphor after which this *prakaraṇa* is named. When someone, on a dark night, waves a firebrand, we see patterns evidently created by the waving light. The patterns as such are not real, but only seem to exist momentarily because the firebrand is in motion. Just so, the seeming objects of our senses are unreal. Only a sort of agitation of thought produces them.

We must be careful not to press this metaphor too far, however. Whatever Gauḍapāda may have thought, later Advaitins will want to insist that the authentic pure consciousness (*Ātman*) is never really agitated, so even to speak of a waving or movement of thought is to speak of what is itself mere illusion. Śaṅkara, in commenting, remarks that a perceiver and the things perceived are only a vibration of thought, a vibration that is itself mere appearance and is based on ignorance.

There is, of course, a problem here. To say that empirical objects are as insubstantial as the patterns of a waving stick is clear enough, but when a firebrand waves we *know* how this is happening; we know, even if we cannot see him or her, that someone is waving it. If consciousness is not "really" waving at all, the firebrand image does not help us to determine why there seems to be such a waving. To say that objects are illusions is intelligible, but we seem to be left with the idea that they are illusions of an illusion, and we would like to know the source of that creative illusion.

Perhaps it is in recognition of this dilemma that verse 52 concedes that such illusions are always finally incomprehensible because we can find no effective cause for them.

Incidentally, the firebrand image was widely popular. It appears, for instance, in the *Maitrāyanīya Upaniṣad* and in the Buddhist *Laṅkāvatāra Sūtra*, and some scholars think it was developed by an Aupaniṣada school even before Gauḍapāda.[38]

XI. VERSES 53–54

{The apparent world could not really be produced by either substance or the insubstantial.}

53. Substance [if it exists] may cause substance, and something insubstantial may be the cause of something else of the same kind, but neither substance nor the insubstantial are suitable categories for entities.
54. The mind is not produced from material things and does not itself produce such things. The wise, therefore, are driven to a doctrine of the non-occurrence of causation.

Those who believe in causality would have to admit that a substance could cause or be caused only by another substance. Similarly, something insubstantial might be produced only by another of its kind. But how are we to explain the arising of substantial things when the only reality is *Ātman*, which is not substantial? And if we were to hold that the true mind or spirit (*Ātman*) were itself merely the product of our physical bodies, this would mean that the insubstantial was produced by substance.

This argument sounds strange to people who have learned that Western philosophy has placed "substance" in a dubious category, and who have no trouble with the idea that our thoughts are functions of a brain, but Gauḍapāda believed that concrete things cannot be produced by mind or mind by concrete things. His conclusion is that no theory of origination is tenable: all must therefore be unborn; *ajātivāda* is the truth.

It may be worth noting that Gauḍapāda's route to this conclusion can be roughly mapped. As early as the *Udāna* of the Pali scriptures we find the concept of *ajāti* applied to some mysterious ground of hope that is somehow different from the world of things that are "born" and therefore perish.[39] By the arising of Mahayana Buddhism we find this idea widely applied to all that appears in the world (although *anutpāda* is a synonym often preferred to *ajāti*) with the attendant idea that all entities are *māyā*, illusions, that only appear to be produced. *Prajñāpāramitā* texts repeat the refrain that no entity (*dharma*) is ever produced or annihilated.[40] Nāgārjuna picked this theme up and developed it influentially in such works as his *Mūla-mādhyamakakārikā*, but it was the Vijñānavāda school that pursued it in a way that most clearly anticipates Gauḍapāda, for its primal reality, *citta-mātra* (Mind only) is virtually indistinguishable from Gauḍapāda's *Ātman*.

XII. VERSES 55–56

{It is false belief in causation that promotes its illusory appearance.}

55. So long as a person believes in cause and effect, these will seem to occur; but when one abandons belief in causes and effects, they vanish entirely.
56. So long as one is possessed by notions of cause and effect, the cycle of birth, death, and rebirth persists. When one no longer believes in causation, the cycle is ended.

Śaṅkara's comment is that so long as confidence in causation is not destroyed the world is eternally present. But if that confidence is overcome, the world is not to be found anywhere because its "cause" has perished.

These verses are simple and direct, and need no amplification. The entire world of cause and effect is an illusion that depends for its continuation on our naive faith in it. To see and accept with all one's heart and mind that no production, birth, or arising ever occur is to dispel forever the illusion of the world.

XIII. VERSES 57–70

{The "real" is eternal; so apparent beginnings are unreal, like a dream or a conjuror's trick.}

57. Everything in ordinary experience has a beginning and is therefore not eternal. By contrast, whatever really exists is without beginning and therefore is also endless.
58. Things are said to begin, but their beginning is

not real: rather, it is like an illusion—but an illusion that itself does not really exist.

59. A sprout that grows from an illusory seed must itself be an illusion, and it therefore cannot properly be said to be either permanent or even temporary. The same is true of other things.
60. One simply cannot apply the terms "eternal" or "noneternal" to objects that never really begin to exist. When words fail, one cannot employ distinctions.
61. Just as the mind, when we are dreaming, moves in the illusion of duality, so even in the waking state duality is an illusion presented by the mind.
62. In dreams the non-dual mind undoubtedly appears to be divided. Similarly, in wakefulness too the non-dual seems to be divided.
63. The creatures we seem to see in dreams, whether womb-born or born of moisture, moving everywhere...
64. are to be seen only in the dreamer's mind and do not exist apart from it. So, too, even the dreamer's mind itself is only imagined to have an independent existence.
65. It is the same with womb- or moisture-born creatures seen in our waking state, moving everywhere...
66. They can be seen only by the mind of the wakeful person, and apart from it they have no existence. And the wakeful mind itself is only imagined to have independent reality.
67. Both perceiver and perceived are established by the perceiving act alone. What, then, is independently real? Nothing! Individual minds are devoid of marks of reality and are imagined by their own thoughts.
68. As dream-produced individuals [*jīvas*] are born and die, so all individuals are and yet are not.
69. As a conjuror's individual is born and dies, so all individuals are and yet are not.
70. As a person created by [yogic] magic is born and dies,so all persons are and yet are not.

In verse 58 the word we have translated "things" is *dharmas*, and may be a direct reference to the early Buddhist concept that all observable entities are composed of *dharmas* (or, in Pali, *dhammas*), elements of matter or energy that are minute in dimension and brief in duration. The main point of this analysis was to emphasize that all persons and things are transient and composite, lacking ability to sustain themselves. The Mahāyāna tradition eventually moved away from this analysis, however, on the grounds of its unintelligibility, which entailed the difficulty of saying how composite things so constructed could be said to attain *nirvāṇa* since this is not composite, not alterable, not transient, and not finite. The main Mahāyāna alternative was to claim that *samsāra* is really *nirvāṇa*, the difference between the two being merely a matter of perception. Gauḍapāda's discussion seems to reflect this position.

Samsāra, says Gauḍapāda, is really illusion. *Māyā* had originally meant a kind of power, but came to mean a power to deceive and, finally, deception or illusion itself: "Māyā ne désigne plus un pouvoir, comme dans la vieille notion héritées des temps védiques, puis exploitée par les religions sectaires; ce mot connote l'erreur qui n'existe qu'autant que la vérité se trouve méconnue, mais s'évanouit devant la vérité acquise."[41]

This use of *māyā* became authoritative in both Mahāyāna and Advaita Vedānta as the only way to reconcile our empirical experience with the conviction that reality is singular and indivisible. It raised a new problem, however. As R. C. Pandeya remarks: "Whether that illusion itself is illusory or not can never be adequately explained—since if it is not illusory, then it does in no way differ from the Absolute, but if it is illusory, we require another illusion to make it illusory."[42]

In commenting on verse 60, Śaṅkara observes that illusory things cannot be analyzed or categorized with such terms as "eternal" or "transitory." Words like those connote a reality, and cannot be applied meaningfully to what does not exist except as fantasy.

As verses 63–67 contend, we all recognize that dream entities exist only in the dreamer's mind. We should as readily see that even objects perceived when we are awake exist only in our mind. If objects could somehow be perceived (or their existence verified) *apart from* our being conscious of them, then we might argue for their independent reality. But it is only through consciousness that we know anything, and Gauḍapāda therefore thinks it reasonable to say that everything we "know" depends on our consciousness and exists only within it. But he goes further. Even our individual consciousness exists only through its content, which defines it as ours. It, too, is not a real, objective, self-sustaining fact. Thus the mind of each of us, and the objects in those minds, are mutually dependent—neither mind nor content is finally "real" in itself. Both must, in some way, depend on something more fundamental, and this, of course, is the supreme *Ātman*.

The last three verses suggest that the life-story of any individual is no more about reality than would be the story of a dream person, or one "created" by an illusionist on stage or, off stage, by the magical-mystical manipulations of a great yogin.

XIV. VERSES 71–74

{Nothing is born. All is of mind, and objectivity is false.}

71. No individual entity is born: no such beginning ever really takes place. This is the highest truth: nothing whatever is originated.
72. The duality of subject and object is only an agitation of the mind itself. The mind is unrelated to any object. Thus it is said to be always unattached.
73. Whatever depends on empirical experience does not really exist. It seems to exist only within that empirical experience on which it is dependent.
74. So everything that ordinary experience judges to be unoriginated is not really so; dependent things arise in ordinary experience.

Verse 71 repeats a statement made in an earlier *kārikā* (III.48) and may be considered the summary of Gauḍapāda's basic doctrine of *ajātivāda*. Although Karmarkar claims that Gauḍapāda is here attacking Buddhist notions of origination, it must be admitted that he merely follows the lead of Mādhyamika and Vijñānavāda in dismissing earlier teachings.

Verse 72 tells us that duality is merely imagined. In truth there is no valid distinction to be made between subject and object, knower and known. Gauḍapāda is not clear about how such an imagination can arise when ultimate consciousness (Brahman) is perfect but, as Śaṅkara notes, Gauḍapāda is concerned simply to make the point that only something that is limited by alien entities can be said to "relate" to anything, and since *Ātman* is the sole reality, it cannot relate or be attached to any object. It is free from such limitations, utterly absolute.

There is debate about the correct rendering of verse 73. *Paratantra*, in the second half, may very well mean "other schools of thought," and if this is Gauḍapāda's meaning, the last section of this *kārikā* may better be translated: "It (that is, the empirical datum) may be considered really to exist by other schools of philosophy, but in fact it does not."

A problem here is, of course, that even the relation of *guru* to disciple seems to be a duality. Critics ask, for whom did Gauḍapāda write his books? If he knew that *Ātman* is all and is undivided, and that nothing exists outside it to be instructed, how can teaching take place? Śaṅkara's response was that the relation of teacher and taught is, indeed, only imagined, and when the teaching has done its work the duality dissolves: the taught is then not other than the teacher, and there is no teaching. This is an "explanation" likely to convince only the already converted.

Verse 74 also presents difficulties for the translator. It could mean that even the concept "unoriginated" is a product of imagination, useful only to refute the teaching of origination in rival schools. Reality (Brahman) itself defies all categorization.

Some commentators, including Śaṅkara, have believed that Gauḍapāda is responding here to the objection that if all things are illusions, scriptures and gurus must also be illusions. This means that all Gauḍapāda's authorities are *māyā* and can support nothing! He is like a man who murders his mother to prove his parentage! The response that Gauḍapāda makes here is disarming. Language is always inadequate to discuss the highest levels of truth, and it is inevitable that even terms like "unborn" belong to that inadequacy and cannot therefore really describe Brahman. Scriptures and *gurus* are certainly part of the realm of illusion, but they are those parts of it that break the spell of the illusion!

It may be worth noting that verses 73 and 74 show unmistakable Vijñānavāda influence in the use of such technical terms as *kalpita*, *paratantra*, and *paramārtha*.

XV. VERSES 75–84

{To grasp the truth is to be liberated from dualism and birth, and from the sorrow, fear, and attachment they bring. It is to know oneself to be unmoving, undivided, unborn, and self-luminous.}

75. Where there is conviction about the unreality of things there is no experience of duality. Whoever understands the unreality of duality is free from it, for its cause has been destroyed.
76. A mind that is not associated with causes, whether these are superior, inferior, or middling, is not born. In the absense of a cause, how could there be an effect?
77. Since the mind is free from birth or any causal relation, everything else is also unoriginated; there is no duality.
78. If we understand true causelessness, and find no cause,we achieve a state without sorrow, desire, or fear.
79. If the mind is attached to unreal objects, it pursues such things. When it realizes that these

objects are unreal, it turns back from them and escapes attachment.

80. A mind thus turned back and inactive is, indeed, without movement. This is the condition of the enlightened ones: unconditioned, unborn, and non-dual.
81. Unborn, sleepless, dreamless, this enlightened mind is self-illuminating. By its very nature it is forever luminous.
82. But if a mind turns toward individual objects, it loses bliss and discovers suffering. The Lord is not, then, easily recovered.
83. [This is because] the misguided person conceals reality with speculation whether it is, is not, is and is not, or neither is nor is not. Or he wonders whether reality moves or is still, is both moving and still, or is neither.
84. These are the four logical alternatives by which people try to understand. That person is all-knowing who recognizes that the luminous one is not to be grasped by such speculation.

Commenting on verses 75 and 76, Śaṅkara explains that "superior" causes are religious behaviors appropriate to a person's class and stage of life. If one has overcome crass desires and lives according to her or his *dharma* (duty) it is supposed, in orthodox theory, that rebirth will introduce the delights of heaven, or at least a more advantageous rebirth. "Middling" causes are similar *dharmic* or dutiful behaviors mixed with irreligious or inappropriate (*adharmic*) ones. Such a blend may produce rebirth among humans on earth, but not necessarily an advantageous one. "Inferior" causes are quite *adharmic* or irreligious and will lead to rebirth in a less desirable state, perhaps as a beast or insect, or even in hell.

The point of these verses is that the entire system of *karma* (consequences) and *samsāra* (rebirth) is brought to nothing for the person who sees that reality is not divided in any way. For such a person there is neither cause nor effect, act nor consequence. The mad illusion of rebirth and redeath is ended.

Verse 77 carries us further. The enlightened person has not only stepped beyond his or her own prospects of another illusory rebirth: since all objects are actually creations of imagination, the liberated mind abandons also the making of such spurious entities. In the end there is only *Ātman* itself, the unborn and eternal reality.

According to verse 78, in the illuminated mind which has no more belief in causes, there is also no ground for the disturbing passions—sorrow, elation, desire, fear, hope or despair. Equanimity is the rule.

This line of thought continues in verses 79 and 80. The ignorant imagine objects and then uselessly pursue these phantoms. The wise understand that there is nothing to pursue, and so attain the great state of Brahman, unconditioned by any object or circumstance, unoriginated and undying, and never torn between impulses or images.

But, as verse 81 implies, the enlightenment of the wise cannot be learned or derived from a source other than itself. It is intrinsically luminous and self-declarative. It depends on nothing. When barriers of ignorance (themselves mere illusions) are brought down, wisdom simply *is*, eternal and self-sustaining.

But (verse 82) the mind that creates and clings to particular things loses its tranquility, and *Ātman* ("the Lord" in our text) is lost to view.

In the final two verses Gauḍapāda lists here the four standard propositions of the kind of logic Nāgārjuna had used so effectively to demonstrate the failure of all propositions and concepts. Gauḍapāda is not, of course, attacking Nāgārjuna—indeed, his intention is similar to the Buddhist's. But where Nāgārjuna laboriously showed that all four logical possibilities invariably led to contradiction if pursued far enough, Gauḍapāda simply says that those who try to reduce truth to one of them wastes precious time, for *Ātman*, the single truth, is outside the range of logic.

Ānandagiri, in what seems to be an effort to rescue Gauḍapāda from the charge of heretical influence, says that the party represented by the "is" option is the Vijñānavāda, the "is and is not" refers to the Jains, and "neither is nor is not" belongs to Mādhyamika.

XVI. VERSES 85–86

{Non-dual consciousness is natural and is the highest value.}

85. If one attains omniscient non-dual wisdom in its fullness, appropriate for a Brahmin, without beginning, middle, or end, what more could one want?
86. This Brahmin discipline is said to be a natural means of introverted tranquility, since nature itself is under control. He who understands this may attain peace.

These verses bring together some interesting terms. Omniscience and non-dual consciousness are explicitly related to the attainment appropriate for a Brahmin. Does this mean, as some have said, that Gauḍapāda is clearly repudiating Buddhism here, showing his unqualified allegiance for the Hindu classification of society into "castes" and for Vedānta? Certainly this is possible, but we must remember that some Buddhist writing often spoke of the "authentic" Brahmin as one who reached that elevated state by the quality of life rather than by birth, and Gauḍapāda may, therefore, be saying here that a state of non-dual consciousness, such as that sought in some forms of Mahāyāna Buddhism, is the true qualification for the term "Brahmin."

In verse 86 we find a word, *vipra*, that often means "Brahmin" associated with the word *vinaya*, which means discipline but was probably more commonly part of the Buddhist vocabulary than the Hindu. Here again, then, we may have the uniting of an orthodox title with a heterodox term, as if to convert one faction to the other or simply to merge the two. On the other hand, *vipra* may mean no more than "inspired" or "wise" so the translation of it as "Brahmin," although probably correct, is not certainly so.

These verses tell us that with nature controlled by natural means (that is, without the aid of anything that comes from outside the subject) contentless and therefore indivisible consciousness arises spontaneously through the introversion of one's attention. The result is tranquility which, if accepted as our true and complete essence, leads to peace.

XVII. VERSES 87–89

{We ordinarily experience three kinds of consciousness, and our knowledge is dualistic. But to understand these matters is to become enlightened.}

87. A waking state may be acknowledged in which duality entailing actual objects is envisioned. There is also a dreaming state where none of the imagined objects are tangible.
88. And there is a further state, traditionally called dreamless sleep, wherein neither object nor images can be found. The enlightened ones affirm knowledge, the object known, and that which should be known.
89. When the trio of knowledge and its kinds of content are understood in the correct order, omniscience spontaneously awakens in a person of great intellect.

In a curious sequence that has caused commentators and translators some difficulty, Gauḍapāda reminds us that there are three forms of consciousness in regular experience: wakeful, dreaming, and dreamless sleep. Then he appears to relate to them three ways of conceiving of the experience of knowledge: there is generally acknowledged to be a knowing, objects known, and *vijñeyam*. Now, this term commonly means "knowable," but one wonders then what distinguishes it from "objects known" (*jñeyam*). The clue may be that *vijñeyam* can also mean "what ought to be known" or *discriminating* knowledge in which truth is clearly separated from error. If we give such an interpretation to it here, it is possible to make sense of the passage. As there are three states of consciousness that everyone experiences, so there are three aspects of understanding that the wise acknowledge: knowing itself, the particular objects or content of knowledge, and—above all and distinct from the others—the state of true, discriminating knowing. Paradoxically, this last, when perfected, issues in a state like dreamless sleep in which no objects are discriminated at all.

Gauḍapāda assures us that if we manage to distinguish clearly the significance of these three aspects of the experience of knowing, putting each in its proper place in an hierarchy, the reward will be the attainment of the final and highest mode: the light of the knowledge that has abandoned objects will dawn in us spontaneously—if we are of sufficient intellectual capacity.

XVIII. VERSE 90

{One may be taught that there are things to be realized, others to be avoided, and yet others to be appropriated or rendered ineffective, but only the first of these is "real."}

90. From the Agrayāna we learn what ought to be avoided, what ought to be realized, what ought to be appropriated, and what ought to be rendered ineffective. Except that which ought to be realized, these are all traditionally recognized as figments of mundane perception.

Since the term Agrayāna was sometimes used as a synonym for Buddhism, some commentators have seen Gauḍapāda as acknowledging here his dependence on that tradition. This is possible, but it should be understood that the word may mean no more than "preliminary" or "fundamental" teaching, and I am inclined to believe that this is its significance here. If so, Gauḍapāda tells us that it is already well known that some things are to be avoided, something is to be realized, other things must be appropriated or used, and yet others made powerless. But what are these things?

If Śaṅkara is correct, we are to avoid the usual contents of mundane experience—things encountered or forgotten in wakefulness, dreams, and dreamless sleep. It is the Absolute (Brahman or *Ātman*) that is to be realized, and as a means to these ends it is *sādhāna*, or spiritual discipline, that is to be appropriated. Passions, especially attachment, hatred and delusion, are to be rendered impotent.

XIX. VERSES 91–95

{So multiplicity is unreal but produces anxiety if we believe in it. The wise seek a non-dual consciousness that is beyond the grasp of the worldly.}

91. Everything should be known to be, by nature, without a beginning, like space. No multiplicity exists anywhere.
92. All things are, by their true nature, established as *Ādibuddha*. Whoever rests content with this is able to achieve immortality.
93. All entities are intrinsically peaceful, unoriginated and perfectly free from anxiety. They are always the same and are not different from each other. They are unborn, identical and perfect.
94. But there is never peace for those who believe in otherness; those who affirm a doctrine of individuality sink into separateness and are traditionally described as pitiful.
95. Those, on the other hand, who wish to be established in the unborn sameness, whoever they are, are indeed persons of great understanding in the world. The world in general does not penetrate such understanding.

These verses summarize the essence of the entire work. Multiplicity is an illusion, for nothing really comes into being and nothing is destroyed. This is because the true essence of whatever is real is *Ādibuddha*, primal, pure truth. To know this and to rest content with it is to dissolve our own sense of spurious otherness and thus to become not different from the singular immortal itself. But to the degree that we stubbornly believe in individuality or particularity, we doom ourselves to continuing ignorance and delusion.

All is one. Therefore sensory experience of objects is false. In thus interpreting the meaning of Upaniṣadic wisdom Gauḍapāda establishes the basis on which radical non-dualism in India was to build. He has chosen to declare one experience alone as valid: that of non-discriminative consciousness in which awareness of objects is lost.

It may be instructive to note that predecessors who had also tried to be faithful to the Upaniṣads had not always found it possible or necessary to reach quite so devastating a view about the nature of worldly objects. As a means of setting Gauḍapāda's teaching in perspective we may outline briefly an alternative, that of the undatable but certainly earlier Bhartṛ-Prapañca. None of this man's own writing remains to us, but he was quoted by Śaṅkara and others and from various references Professor M. Hiriyanna has constructed an interesting summary of his teaching.[43]

Bhartṛ-Prapañca agreed with Gauḍapāda and Śaṅkara that the Upaniṣads teach monism. However, his was a form of monism that allowed a kind of reality to the objects of ordinary experience. One might say that for him, as for St. Paul, within the ultimate reality itself particular beings "live and move and exist."[44]

For Gauḍapāda Brahman is real, and particular entities only appear to be so. This is a doctrine of the unreality of difference. In contrast, Bhartṛ-Prapañca taught that particular things and persons are quite real, although dependent on Brahman and existing only as a sort of mode of Brahman's being—a doctrine of identity in difference (*bhedābheda*).

There appear to have been four examples offered of the meaning of such a view. (1) The material cause and its effect. For example, clay and the pot made from it: while the pot exists, it has reality, yet it is not fundamentally "other" than the clay to whose amorphous character it will finally return. (2) Substance and mode. This is the example most commonly attributed to Bhartṛ-Prapañca. An example would be the ocean and its waves. (3) Whole and part. Each branch of a tree is unique and real, yet it participates in the wholeness of the tree. (4) Universal and particular. Each individual cow is real, yet is a cow because it participates in the universal "cowness" of its kind.

Bhartṛ-Prapañca taught that each *jīva* or individual person is a real transformation of Brahman. Each of us is quite literally as real in our uniqueness as Brahman, the universal. The difference between us and Brahman is that we are temporary manifestations, Brahman is eternal, and we are dependent on Brahman, but Brahman's reality is independent. Our ignorance, then, is not in believing in our individuality, but in failing to see our ontological dependence.

Bhartṛ-Prapañca held that perception, when validly performed, was a true *pramāṇa* (means of legitimate knowledge) and that this implies that our perception of objects validates the actual existence of them. He also held that scriptures testified in many places to the reality of objects.

It seems clear, from the frequency with which he is quoted, that Bhartṛ-Prapañca was once held in high esteem, and it is perhaps surprising that his view was so completely overshadowed by that of Gauḍapāda. Aspects of it were revived, of course, in the later philosophy of Rāmānuja, but until then Gauḍapāda's triumph may be attributed to Śaṅkara's dominance as a controversialist and the relentless human quest for simplicity. Maybe many were persuaded by Gauḍapāda's insistence that only the "pitiful" worldling could continue to see any measure of reality in otherness.

XX. VERSES 96–99

{Only non-dual consciousness is detached from objects.}

96. The unoriginated knowledge is thought of as not making contact with objects which are them-

selves unoriginated. As it lacks such contact, it is said to be unconditioned.

97. If a difference of even the slightest degree is affirmed by the unwise, there is no consistent detachment and therefore no penetrating of the veil of illusion.
98. All beings are by nature free of accretions and are unstained. The Masters say they are free and pure light from the first.
99. According to the enlightened one, understanding never touches objects, and nothing touches understanding. The Buddha has not said this.

Since all is one, and that one is pure consciousness, there are no real relationships. Reality is not impinged upon or conditioned by anything, for it is indivisible and invulnerable. But if we persist in holding a view that attributes even a meager independence to particular things, our understanding is clouded. Such a view simply precludes the attainment of unity in consciousness. Reality is free, pure light, and nothing else. Śaṅkara points out that even to speak of overcoming delusion may lead the unwary to think that the delusion is a real something that co-exists with Brahman. This is not so. Nothing is ever truly related to anything, and there is therefore no real obstruction.

The enigmatic end of verse 99 has already been discussed in the introduction. Let us simply remind ourselves that it may mean either that this final truth of unrelatedness was not taught by the Buddha, or that the Buddha did not teach anything else!

XXI. VERSE 100

{The highest state of consciousness is to be honored without qualification.}

100. Having attained the supreme state which is profound, birthless, void of distinctions, imperishable and always the same, we offer it all possible honor.

This final verse should be seen as a conventional honoring of truth. It is, perhaps, a little ironic that there is a sort of logical inconsistency in it: if Gauḍapāda had attained the non-dual state in which neither independent subject nor object persists, and in which action is seen to be unreal, the action of honoring the truth as if it were objective is a little strange. But convention often overrides logic.

Notes

1. Ānandagiri's *Tīkā on Māṇḍūkyopaniṣad*, IV. 1 in *Māṇḍūkyopaniṣad with Gauḍapāda's Kārikā, Śaṅkara's Bhāṣya and Ānandagiri's Tīkā* (Poona: Anandāśrama Sanskrit Series, no. 10, 1897).

2. Max Walleser, *Der Ältere Vedānta: Geschichte, Kritik und Lehr* (Heidelberg: Carl Winter's Universitätsbuchhandlung, 1910), 3f.

3. A. L. Basham, *The Origin and Development of Classical Hinduism* (New York: Oxford University Press, 1991).

4. Karl H. Potter, *Prespposition̈s of India's Philosophies* (Englewood Cliffs, N.J.: Prentice-Hall, Inc., 1963), 93.

5. Raghunath Damodar Karmarkar, *Gauḍapāda-Kārikā* (Poona: Bhandarkar Oriental Research Institute, 1953), 148.

6. *Saddharmalaṅkāvatāra-Sūtram*, ed. P. L. Vaidya (Darbhanga: The Mithila Institute of Post-Graduate Studies and Research in Sanskrit Learning, 1963), lines 20ff., p. 58.

7. Surendranath Dasgupta, *A History of Indian Philosophy*, vol. 2 (Cambridge: Cambridge University Press, 1963), 478.

8. For this careful translation of a difficult passage I am indebted to Professor Ronald Morton Smith of the University of Toronto, who allowed me to see an unpublished manuscript. He has followed the Sanskrit as exactly as English syntax allows.

9. Ibid.

10. P. V. Bapat, *2500 Years of Buddhism* (Delhi: Ministry of Information and Broadcasting, 1956), 307.

11. S. C. Chakravarti, *The Philosophy of the Upanishads* (Delhi: Seema Publications, 1980), 198.

12. Cf., for an example, C. T. Kenghe, "Nāgārjuna and Gauḍapāda," *Aligarh Journal of Oriental Studies*, vol. 3, no. 1 (Spring 1986), 11-16.

13. Nāgārjuna, *Mādhyamaka-Kārikās*, VII.34.

14. Vidhushekhara Bhattacharya (ed. and tr.), *The Āgamaśāstra of Gauḍapāda* (Calcutta: The University of Calcutta Press, 1943), xxxii.

15. R. D. Ranade, *Vedānta: The Culmination of Indian Thought* (Bombay: Bharatiya Vidya Bhavan, 1970), 43.

16. Ronald Morton Smith, "Power in Ancient India," *Annals of the Bhandarkar Oriental Research Institute*, vol. 39, parts 1–2 (January–April 1958), 9.

17. Vincent A. Smith, *The Early History of India*, 4th edition (Oxford: Oxford University Press, 1924), 370.

18. Cf., Michel Foucault, *The Order of Things: An Archeology of the Human Sciences* (New York: Random House, 1970), and *Power/ Knowledge: Selected Interviews and Other Writings 1972–1977*, ed. Colin Gordon (New York: Pantheon, 1980).

19. T. M. P. Mahadevan, *Gauḍapāda: A Study in Early Vedānta* (Madras: University of Madras, 1960), 113.

20. Ibid., 82.

21. Ibid., 83.

22. S. Venkatasubbiah, "The Māṇḍūkyopaniṣad and Gauḍapāda," *The Indian Antiquary*, vol. 42 (1933), 181–93.

23. Vidhushekhar Bhattacharya, "The Māṇḍūka Upaniṣad and the Gauḍapāda Kārikās," *The Indian Historical Quarterly*, vol. 1, no. 1 (March 1925), 119–24.

24. Amar Nath Ray, "The Māṇḍūkya Upaniṣad and the Kārikās of Gauḍapāda," *The Indian Historical Quarterly*, vol. 14, no. 3 (1938), 566–67.

25. Karmarkar, *Gauḍapāda-Kārikā*, xxxi.

26. Caterina Conio, *The Philosophy of Māṇḍūkya Kārikā* (Varanasi: Bharatiya Vidya Prakashan, 1971), 11.

27. There is some doubt whether Śaṅkara actually wrote the commentary attributed to him, but since the attribution is traditional we shall refer to it as his. All further references to it will relate to specific verses of Gauḍapāda's *Kārikā*, and the source is: *Māṇḍūkyopaniṣad with Gauḍapāda's Kārikā, Śaṅkara's Bhāṣya and Ānandagiri's Tikā* (Poona: Anandāśrama Sanskrit Series,35, 4 10, 1897).

28. Cf. *Laṅkāvatāra*, "Sangathakam," verses 273–77.

29. Andrew O. Fort, "Dreaming in Advaita Vedānta," *Philosophy East and West*, vol. 35, no. 4 (October 1985), p. 377.

30. Paul Masson-Oursel, *Esquisse d'une Histoire de la Philosophie Indienne* (Paris: Paul Geuthner, 1923), 211.

31. William M. Indich, *Consciousness in Advaita Vedānta* (Delhi: Motilal Banarsidass, 1980), 123.

32. Karmarkar, *Gauḍapāda-Kārikā*, 115–16.

33. Candrakirti, *Mādhamakavṛtti*, XI. 7-8, Louis de la Vallée Poussin (ed.) (St. Petersburg: The Academy of Sciences of the U.S.S.R., 1903), 444.

34. Ānandagiri, *Tīkā on Gauḍapāda's Kārikā* III:36, in *Māṇḍūkyopaniṣad with Gauḍapāda's Kārikā, Śaṅkara's Bhāṣya and Ānandagiri's Tīkā* (Poona: Anandāśrama Saṇskrit Series, no. 10, 1897).

35. Karmarkar, *Gauḍapāda-Kārikā*, 123.

36. Cf. Candrakirti, *Mādhamaka-Vṛtti*, ed. Louis de la Vallée Poussin (St. Petersburg: The Academy of Sciences, 1903), 444.

37. Karmarkar, *Gauḍapāda-Kārikā*, 125.

38. Cf. A. Berriedale Keith, *A History of Sanskrit Literature* (Oxford: Oxford University Press, 1920), 476.;and M. Winternitz, *History of Indian Literature*, vol. 3, part 2, tr. Subhadra Jha (Delhi: Motilal Banarsidass, 1889), 484.

39. *Khuddaka Nikāya*, vol. 1, p. 163, line 10 (Bihar: Pali Publication Board, 1959).

40. E.g., *the Perfection of Wisdom in Seven Hundred Lines*, partly translated by Edward Conze in *Thirty Years of Buddhist Studies* (London: Bruno Cassirer, 1967), 195.

41. Masson-Oursel, *Esquisse d'une Histoire de la Philosophie Indienne*, 195.

42. R. C. Pandeya, "The Mādhyamika Philosophy: A New Approach," *Philosophy East and West*, vol. 14, no. 1 (April 1964).

43. M. Hiriyanna, "Bhartṛ-Prapañca: An Old Vedāntin," *The Indian Antiquary*, vol. 53, 1 (April 1924), 77–86.

44. Acts 17:28.

Bibliography

Arapura, J. G. "Māyā and the Discourse about Brahman," in Mervyn Sprung (ed.) *The Problem of Two Truths in Buddhism and Vedānta*. Dordrecht, Holland: D. Reidel Publishing Co., 1973.

Bapat, P. V. *2500 Years of Buddhism*. Delhi: Ministry of Information and Broadcasting, 1956.

Basham, A. L. *The Origins and Development of Classical Hinduism*. New York: Oxford University Press, 1991.

Betty, L. Stafford. "A Death-Blow to Śaṅkara's Non-Dualism? A Dualist Refutation." *Religious Studies*, vol. 12, no. 3 (September 1976), 381–90.

Bharadwaja, V. K. "Rationality, Argumentation and Embarrassment: A Study of Four Logical Alternatives (Catuṣoki) in Buddhist Logic." *Philosophy East and West*, vol. 34, no. 3 (July 1984), 303–16.

Bhattacharya, Kamaleswar. *L'Ātman-Brahman dans le Bouddhisme Ancien*. Paris: École Française d'Extrême-Orient, 1973.

Bhattacharya, Vidhushekhara (ed. and tr.). *The Āgama-śāstra of Gauḍapāda*. Calcutta: University of Calcutta Press, 1943.

———. "Gauḍapāda." *The Indian Historical Quarterly*, vol. 14 (June 1938), 392–98.

———. "The Māṇḍūkya Upaniṣad and the Gauḍapāda Kārikās," *The Indian Historical Quarterly*, vol. 1 (March 1925), 119–24.

Bhattacharyya, Krishna Chandra. *Studies in Vedāntism.* Calcutta: The University of Calcutta Press, 1909.

Bishop, Donald (ed.). *Indian Thought: An Introduction.* New York: John Wiley and Sons, 1975.

Candrakirti. *Mādhyamaka-vṛtti* (ed. Louis de la Vallée Poussin). St. Petersburgh: The Academy of Sciences, 1903–1913.

Chakravarti, S. C. *The Philosophy of the Upanishads.* Delhi: Seema Publications, 1980.

Chatterjee, Satischandra, and Dhirendramodhan Datta. *An Introduction to Indian Philosophy.* Calcutta: University of Calcutta Press, 1968.

Chinmayananda, Swami. *Discourses on Māṇḍūkya Upanishad with Gauḍapāda's Kārikā.* Madras: Chinmaya Publications Trust, 1953.

Cole, Colin A. *Asparśa-Yoga.* Delhi: Motilal Banarsidass, 1982.

Conio, Caterina. *The Philosophy of Māṇḍūkya Kārikā.* Varanasi: Bharatiya Vidya Prakashan, 1971.

Damodaran, K. *Indian Thought: A Critical Survey.* Bombay: Asia Publishing House, 1967.

Dasgupta, Surendranath. *A History of Indian Philosophy,* vol. 2. Cambridge: Cambridge University Press, 1965 and 1969.

Dvivedi, M. N. (tr.). *The Māṇḍūkyopaniṣad with Gauḍa-*

pāda's Kārikās and the Bhāṣya of Śaṅkara. Bombay: Bombay Theosophical Publication Fund, 1894.

Factor, R. Lance. "What is the 'Logic' in Buddhist Logic?" *Philosophy East and West*, vol. 33, no. 2 (April 1983), 184–87.

Fort, Andrew O. "Dreaming in Advaita Vedānta." *Philosophy East and West*, vol. 30, no. 4 (October 1985), 377–86.

Foucault, Michel. *The Order of Things: An Archeology of the Human Sciences.* New York: Random House, 1970.

———. *Power/Knowledge: Selected Interviews and Other Writings 1972–1977*, ed. Colin Gordon. New York: Pantheon, 1980.

Gauḍapāda. *Māṇḍūkyopaniṣad with Gauḍapāda's Kārikā, Śaṅkara's Bhāṣya and Ānandagiri's Tīkā.* Poona: Anandāśrama Sanskrit Series, no. 10, 1897.

Hacker, Paul. *Vivarta: Studien zur Geschichte der Illusionistischen Kosmologie und Erkenntnistheorie der Inder.* Mainz: Akademie der Wissenschaften und der Literatur, 1953.

Hager, Berthold. *Die Entwicklung des Māyā-Begriffes im Indoarischen.* Freiberg: Verlag Wolf Morson, 1983.

Hiriyanna, M. "Bhartṛ-Prapañca: An Old Vedāntin." *The Indian Antiquary*, vol. 53, no 1 (April 1924), 77–86.

Hoang-Sy-Quy, S.J. *Le Moi qui me Dépasse selon le Vedānta.* Saigon: Les Editions Hung Giao Van Dong, n.d.

Indich, William M. "Can the Advaita Vedānta Provide a Meaningful Definition of Absolute Consciousness?"

Philosophy East and West, vol. 30, no. 4 (October 1980), 481–93.

———. *Consciousness in Advaita Vedānta*. Delhi: Motilal Banarsidass, 1980.

Karmarkar, Raghunath Damodar. *Gauḍapāda-Kārikā*. Poona: Bhandarkar Oriental Research Institute, 1953.

Keith, A. Berriedale. *A History of Sanskrit Literature*. Oxford: Oxford University Press, 1920.

Kenghe, C. T. "Nāgārjuna and Gauḍapāda." *Aligarh Journal of Oriental Studies*, vol. 3, no. 1 (Spring 1986), 11–16.

Koller, John M. *The Indian Way*. New York: Macmillan Publishing Co., 1982.

Lacombe, Olivier. *L'Absolu selon le Vedānta*. Paris: Librairie Orientaliste Paul Geuthner, 1966.

Lesimple, Em. (tr.). *Māṇḍūkya Upaniṣad et Kārikā de Gauḍapāda*. Paris: Libraire d'Amerique et d'Orient, 1944.

Loy, David. "Enlightenment in Buddhism and Advaita Vedānta: Are *Nirvāṇa* and *Moksha* the Same?" *International Philosophical Quarterly*, vol. 21 (1982), 64–74.

Mahadevan, T. M. P. *Gauḍapāda: A Study in Early Vedānta*. Madras: The University of Madras Press, 1960.

———. *Preceptors of Avaita*. Secunderabad: Sri Kanchi Kamakoti Śaṅkara Mandir, 1968.

Mainkar, T. G. *The Making of the Vedānta*. Delhi: Ajanta Publications (India), 1980.

Murti, T. R. V. "Saṁvṛti and Paramārtha in Mādhyamaka and Advaita Vedānta," in *The Problem of Two Truths in Buddhism and Vedānta*, ed. Mervyn Sprung. Dordrecht, Holland: D. Reidel Publishing Co., 1973.

Nikhilananda, Swami. *The Māṇḍūkyopaniṣad with Gauḍapāda's Kārikā and Śaṅkara's Commentary.* Mysore: Sri Ramakrishna Ashrama, 1936.

Masson-Oursel, Paul. *Esquisse d'une Histoire de la Philosophie Indienne.* Paris: Paul Geuthner, 1923.

O'Neil, L. Thomas. *Māyā in Śaṅkara.* Delhi: Motilal Banarsidass, 1980.

Pandeya, R. C. "The Mādhyamika Philosophy: A New Approach." *Philosophy East and West*, vol. 14, no. 1 (April 1964), 3–24.

Potter, Karl H. (ed.). *The Encyclopaedia of Indian Philosophies.* Princeton, N.J.: Princeton University Press, 1981.

———. *Presuppositions of India's Philosophies.* Englewood Cliffs, N.J.: Prentice-Hall, 1963.

Radhakrishnan, Sarvepalli. *Indian Philosophy.* New York: The Macmillan Co., 1927.

Raju, P. T. *The Philosophical Traditions of India.* London: George Allen and Unwin, 1971.

Ramaiah, C. *The Problem of Change and Identity in Indian Philosophy.* Tirupati: Sri Venkateswara University Press, 1978.

Ranade, R. D. *A Constructive Survey of Upaniṣadic Philosophy.* Poona: Oriental Book Agency, 1926.

———. *Vedānta: The Culmination of Indian Thought.* Bombay: Bharatiya Vidya Bhavan, 1970.

Rao, K. B. R. *Ontology of Advaita.* Mulki: Vijaya College, 1964.

Rao, M. Srinivasa (tr.). *Māṇḍūkya Upaniṣad with Gauḍapāda's Kārikā and Śaṅkara's Commentary.* Madras: Vedānta Kesari, 1931–1935.

Ray, Amar Nath. "The Māṇḍūkya Upaniṣad and the Kārikās of Gauḍapāda," *The Indian Historical Quarterly,* vol. 14, no. 3 (September 1938), 564–69.

Sahasrabudhe, M. T. *A Survey of the Pre-Śaṅkara Advaita Vedānta.* Poona: University of Poona Press, 1968.

Sarvananda, Swami (tr.). *Māṇḍūkyopaniṣad with a Summary of Gauḍapāda's Kārikās by Swami Tyagisananda.* Madras: Sri Ramakrishna Math, 1964.

Sastri, P. S. *Indian Idealism: Epistemology and Ontology.* Delhi: Bharatiya Vidya Prakashan, 1975.

Sastri, S. R. Krishnamurthi, and Dikshitar, P. V. Sivarama (eds.). *Māṇḍūkyagauḍapādiya with Śaṅkara Bhāṣya and Anubhūtisvarūpācārya's Tippaṇam.* Madras: Sanskrit Education Society, 1978.

Satchidananda, Saraswati. *Māṇḍūkya Rahasya Vivriti: A Commentary on Sri Gauḍapāda's Māṇḍūkya Kārikā.* Holenarsipur: Adhyatma Prakash Karylaya, 1958.

Sharma, B. N. K. *The Brahmasūtras and Their Principal Commentators,* vol. 1. Bombay: Bharatiya Vidya Bhavan, 1971.

Sharma, Chandradhar. *Indian Philosophy: A Critical Survey.* New York: Barnes and Noble, 1962.

Shastri, Prabhu Dutt. *The Doctrine of Māyā in the Philosophy of the Vedānta*. London: Luzac and Co., 1911.

Smith, Ronald Morton. "Power in Ancient India," *Annals of the Bhandarkar Oriental Research Institute*, vol. 38, parts iii–iv (1958), 1–33.

———. "The Early Heresies in the Development of Indian Religion," *Indologica Taurinensia*, vol. 2, (1974), 149–98.

Smith, Vincent A. *The Early History of India*, 4th edition. Oxford: Oxford University Press, 1924.

Venkatasubbiah, A. "The Māṇḍūkyopaniṣad and Gauḍapāda," *The Indian Antiquary*, vol. 62 (1933), 181–93.

Vidyabhusana, S. C. *A History of Indian Logic*. Delhi: Motilal Banarsidass, 1971.

Von Glasenapp, Helmuth. *Vedānta und Buddhismus*. Mainz: Akademie der Wissenschaften und der Literatur, 1950.

Walleser, Max. *Der Ältere Vedānta: Geschichte, Kritik und Lehr*. Heidelberg: Carl Winter's Universitätsbuchhandlung, 1910.

Winternitz, Maurice. *History of Indian Literature*, tr. Subhadra Jha, Delhi: Motilal Banarsidass, 1889.

Index

Ādibuddha, 125
Advaita, xi, xii, 4, 56, 60, 63, 64
Advaita Vedānta, 3, 4; consciousness in, 43, 112; and Gauḍapāda, 21, 23, 34, 40, 57, 64–65, 122; levels of truth in, 66; *māyā* in, 116; non-dualism in, 59, 69, 104; non-origination in, 29, 62; self in, 14; significance in India, 3–4
Āgama-śāstra, 22
Agrayāṇa, 68, 88, 124
Ajāti: arguments for, 71–76; *Gītā*, in, 24; and mundane objects, 62; *Udāna*, in, 113; and universe, 101; *upaniṣads*, in, 26–31
Ajātivāda, 22, 24, 31, 74, 109–110, 113, 118
Ājīvika, 14, 16
Ākāśa, 56
Alātaśānti, xii, 6, 81
Ānanda, 67
Ānandagiri, 4, 5, 94, 105, 110, 121
Anutpāda, 29, 113
Āraṇyaka, 11
Arjuna, 12, 13, 24
Āryan, 9–10
Asparśayoga, 57, 67–68, 94
Ātman: Brahman, identity with, 11, 24, 32, 55, 58, 62–65, 103–104, 117, 125; *Bṛhadāraṇyaka*, in, 34; *citta-mātra*, similarity to, 114; and consciousness, 43, 112; and human selfhood, 11, 20, 56; illusion, creator of, 108; non-duality of, 68, 118; production by, 113; Samkhya, in, 16; *Turya*, as, 61; unborn nature of, 26, 121; unchanging, 48, 56–57, 96
Avatār, 13
Avidyā. *See* Ignorance

Bapat, P. V., 29
Basham, A. L., 12–13
Bhagavad Gītā, 11–12, 24–25, 110
Bhartṛ-Prapañca, 126–127
Bhattacharya, Vidhushekhara, 21, 22–23, 34, 46–47, 98
Bhāvaviveka, 5
Brahman: *ātman*, identity with, 20, 32, 62, 104;consciousness, as, 53, 61, 66–67, 102; immutability of, 43, 62, 64–65, 73–74, 105, 111; impersonal, 11–13; and *māyā*, 63; nonduality of, 67, uncreative, 55, 58, 108–109; universality, 40, 56, 71, 125, 128; upaniṣads, in, 25–28
Bṛhadāraṇyaka, 25, 26, 34, 37, 103
Buddha, 23, 35–36, 38–39, 44, 66, 94, 109, 128

Buddhism: ajāti, in, 104, 113, 118; decline of, 36, 38–39; eightfold path, 15; Gauḍapāda and, 21–24, 34, 36, 40,57, 61, 64–65, 122, 124; *samsāra*, 104; *śruti*, rejection of, 35

Candrakirti, 99
Causation: Gauḍapāda's refutation of, 71–76, 82–89, 95–105, 113– 114, 119–121; Mādhyamika refutation of, 30–31
Chakravarti, S. C., 29
Chāndogya, 34
Citta-mātra, 32, 40, 114
Conio, Caterina, 49
Consciousness: contentless, 20, 43, 58, 67–68, 85, 102, 128; non-dual, 112, 122, 125–126; reality as, 3, 24, 117; stages of, 59–62, 65, 66, 123–124; upaniṣads, in, 26

Dasgupta, Surendranath, 21, 25
Deussen, Paul, 46
Dharma: duty, as, 13, 14, 120; entity, 113, 116
Dīgha Nikāya, 15

Fort, Andrew O., 61
Foucault, Michel, 38–39

Gauḍapāda: date of, 5; identity, xi, 3–5; relation to Buddhism, xi, xii, 6, 7, 21–40; works attributed, xii, 5–6
Govinda, xi, 3, 5

Hiriyanna, M., 126
Hume, David, 19, 98

Ignorance, 52, 112, 121, 126
Illusion: experience as, 55, 56, 115, 121; superimposition of, 28; world as, 15, 29, 66, 84–86, 105, 110–112. *See also māyā*
Indich, William M., 65

Jainism, 14, 16, 122
Jaspers, Karl, 11
Jīva, 56, 58, 87, 96, 115, 127

Kārikā, 6, 21, 45–48
Karma, 10, 11, 16, 33, 64, 69, 120
Karmarkar, Raghunath Damodar, 21, 22–23, 47, 79, 98–99, 107, 110, 118
Katha, 26
Kṛṣṇa, 12, 13, 24, 25

Laṅkāvatara Sūtra, 23, 55, 112
Liberation, 14, 15, 16, 17. *See also Mokṣa*
Logic: Gauḍapāda's, 42, 71–76, 98–100; Hindu, 107–108; Mādhyamika, 30, 171

Mādhyamika, 29–32, 33, 34, 40, 69, 107, 118, 122
Mahadevan, T. M. P., 21, 40, 41, 43
Māṇḍūkya, xii, 22, 45–49; summary of, 51–70
Māṇḍūkyopaniṣad Kārikā, xii, 6, 22, 45–49
Materialism, 14, 15, 17
Māyā: cause of, 64; *Gītā*, in, 24–25; individuals as, 63, 65; and sensory experience, 24, 31, 63, 116; upaniṣads, in, 25–29; world as, 52–53, 57, 74, 108, 113, 119
Meditation, 16, 30, 43, 58, 67, 68, 71

Mīmāṃsā, 14, 15, 18
Mind: materiality, relation to, 86–88, 113, 115, 117; unborn nature of, 102–103, 110, 119; Vijñānavāda, in, 32–33, 114. *See also citta-mātra*
Mokṣa, 68–69, 104, 105
Mūlamādhyamakārikā, 114
Muṇḍaka, 27
Murti, T. R. V., 21

Nāgārjuna, 30–31, 34, 40, 42, 66–67, 71, 100, 121
Nirguṇa, 64, 110
Nirvāṇa, 30, 31, 69, 116
Niyati, 17
Non-dualism: experience, 56; fearlessness in, 40; Gauḍapāda's, xi, 42, 122, 125–126; *Gītā*, in, 13; illusion of, 86, 87, 115, 119; reason and, 41. *See also advaita*
Non-production, 57, 58, 63, 74, 95. *See also ajāti*
Nyāya, 14, 18, 95

Origination: concession to weakness, as, 66, 85, 109, 118; Nāgārjuna's view of, 31; rejection of, 58, 81, 87, 95, 106, 110, 127–128
Orthodox Systems, 13–20

Pandeya, R. C., 116
Paramārtha-satya, 66
Patañjali, 15
Peace, 33, 67, 69, 88, 89,122, 123, 125
Perception, 17–20, 103, 115, 117, 127
Potter, Karl H., 15
Prajāpati, 11,
Prajñā, 51, 121, 122
Prajñāpāramitā, 113
Prakṛti, 14
Pramāna, xii, 17, 41–44, 127
Praśna, 29
Production: arguments against, 71–76, 82, 96–98, 101, 113; Gauḍapāda's doctrine, 31, 65, 95; illusion of, 57, 86. *See also ajātivāda*
Puruṣa(h), 14, 16, 27, 37

Radhakrishnan, Sarvepalli, 21
Rāmānuja, 28, 74, 75, 127
Ranade, R. D., 34
Ray, Amar Nath, 47
Ṛg Veda, 10, 11, 36, 63

Saguṇa, 64, 110
Samādhi, 57
Sāṃkhya, 14, 15, 95, 98–99
Samsāra, 10, 11, 14, 22, 104–105, 116, 120
Samvṛti-satya, 66
Sautrantika, 107
Self, 11, 14, 15, 16, 20, 27, 34, 53. *See also ātman*
Smith, Ronald Morton, 35
Smith, Vincent A., 36
Subāla, 29
Superimposition, 108–109
Svetāśvatara, 27–29
Śaṅkara: Brahman, concept of, 55; Buddhism, criticism of, 3, 31; causation, 62; commentary on *Alātaśānti*, 53, 68, 94, 99, 100, 102, 107, 112, 116, 120, 125, 128; non-dualism, 27–28, 65; Gauḍapāda, relation to, xi, 43, 63, 127
Śruti, 35, 40, 44, 46, 47
Śūnya, 31, 66, 69
Śūnyatā, 30, 32, 33, 69

Tarka, 42
Theism: *Bhagavad Gītā*, in, 12–13; divine creativity, 52,

Theism *(continued)*
62; Human destiny, 15; *Ṛg Veda*, in, 10, 36–37; *saguṇa-Brahman*, 64; *Svetāśvatara Upaniṣad*, in, 27–29; *upaniṣads*, in, 11
Turya, 51, 53, 61, 64, 66

Unborn: Brahman, 104, 110, 121; and cause-effect theory, 82–89, 97; entities, 58, 81, 95, 102, 106, 125; mind, 102–103, 119, 120. *See also ajāti*
Upaniṣads: authority of, 39, development of, 11, Gauḍapāda's use of, 3, 6, 21, 23–24, 32, 34, 40, 126; non-dualaism in, 19–20. *See also Bṛhadāraṇyaka, Chāndogya, Katha, Māṇḍūkya, Muṇḍaka Praśna*

Vaiśeṣika, 14
Vasubandhu, 5,
Vedas: Āryans in, 9–10; authority of, 3, 32, 35, 39, 109; recovery of, xi
Vedānta. *See* Advaita Vedānta
Venkatasubbiah, A., 46
Vijñānavāda, 29, 32–40, 61, 64, 114, 118, 119, 122
Viṣṇu, 12, 13

Walleser, Max, 4, 46

Yoga, 14, 15, 67–68, 81, 93, 94